Prompt Engineering: The Ultimate Guide

Introduction

Prompt Engineering is an essential discipline to make the most of the power of Artificial Intelligence (AI) models, especially those based on natural language processing (NLP), such as GPT models. While AI systems have become highly sophisticated, the way we interact with them is still crucial to getting accurate and useful results. Here, the concept of "prompt" refers to the request we make to the AI to generate a response or perform a specific task.

The field of prompt engineering is about the art and science of strategically formulating questions, commands, and requests so as to elicit the best possible responses from AI systems. Whether it's answering a simple question, generating creative content, or even automating complex tasks, understanding how to build effective prompts can make all the difference in the performance of an AI model.

This eBook aims to provide a comprehensive understanding of prompt engineering, covering everything from basic concepts to advanced, practical techniques. Throughout the chapters, we'll explore how prompt engineering can be applied in a variety of contexts, such as natural language processing, code generation, creative content creation, and more. We'll also discuss best practices, challenges, and emerging trends in this area, helping you become an expert at optimizing your interactions with AI.

The journey of prompt engineering will not only improve your ability to interact with AI systems more efficiently, but it will also open up new possibilities for automating processes and creating innovative solutions.

Foreword

Prompt Engineering is an emerging and highly relevant area in the field of Artificial Intelligence (AI). While AI models are becoming more powerful, the way we interact with them—the way we formulate **prompts** (commands or requests made to models), remains one of the key determinants of getting useful, accurate, and relevant responses.

This eBook, "Prompt Engineering: The Ultimate Guide," was created to give you a thorough understanding of this essential discipline. Whether you're an AI enthusiast, a tech professional, or someone who wants to learn how to interact more effectively with intelligent systems, this guide will provide you with the tools and knowledge you need to hone your skills in creating prompts.

Throughout the chapters, we will explore the evolution of AI models, from the simplest, rule-based approaches to today's multimodal, self-adaptive systems. We'll cover the theory behind prompt engineering, but above all, we'll focus on **practical examples** and **applicable tips**, so you can implement what you've learned right away.

Prompt engineering isn't just about writing commands for AI; it's about creating effective communication between humans and machines, allowing us to take full advantage of the capabilities of these technologies. In a world increasingly reliant on AI, the skills to construct prompts accurately and strategically are not only useful; are essential.

This guide not only explains the fundamentals but also offers **advanced insights**, covering topics such as prompt customization, continuous learning approaches, the use of multimodal AI, and important ethical considerations. By the end of this eBook, you will have a broad view of prompt engineering and be able to apply this knowledge to improve your interactions with AI models, becoming a true expert in the field.

Welcome to the "Ultimate Guide to Prompt Engineering." I hope you enjoy this learning journey and apply this knowledge to explore the incredible potential that AI has to offer.

Index

1. Introduction
2. Foreword

Chapter 1: Fundamentals of Prompt Engineering

1.1 What are Prompts?
1.2 Difference Between Prompts and Queries
1.3 Types of Language Models and Their Capabilities
1.4 How Does the Prompt Formulation Impact the Response?

Chapter 2: Structure of an Efficient Prompt

2.1 Essential Elements of a Prompt
2.2 How to Formulate a Clear and Objective Prompt
2.3 Specifying Contexts and Details
2.4 Practical Examples of Basic Prompts
2.5 How to Improve the Quality of Prompts with Iteration

Chapter 3: Types of Prompts and Their Applications

3.1 Question Prompts
3.2 Instruction Prompts
3.3 Creative Stimulus Prompts
3.4 Analysis or Explanation Prompts
3.5 Persuasion or Argumentation Prompts
3.6 Comparison Prompts
3.7 How to Choose the Right Prompt Type?

Chapter 4: Advanced Prompt Engineering Techniques

    4.1 Use of Contexts and Examples
    4.2 Chunking
    4.3 Prompt Chaining
    4.4 Few-Shot Learning
    4.5 Using Metadata for Response Refinement
    4.6 Practical Examples of Advanced Techniques
    4.7 Conclusion

Chapter 5: Common Challenges and How to Overcome Them in Prompt Engineering

    5.1 Ambiguity in Prompts
    5.2 Model Knowledge Limitations
    5.3 Superficial or Generic Answers
    5.4 Complex or Ambiguous Sentences
    5.5 Tendency to Predictable or Common Responses
    5.6 How to Overcome Common Challenges: Tips and Best Practices
    5.7 Conclusion

Chapter 6: Optimizing Prompts to Maximize Results

    6.1 What is Prompt Optimization?
    6.2 Techniques to Optimize Prompts
    6.3 Strategies for Obtaining High-Quality Results
    6.4 Adjusting the Tone and Style of the Response
    6.5 Common Mistakes When Creating Prompts and How to Avoid Them
    6.6 Testing and Refining Prompts
    6.7 Conclusion

Chapter 7: Prompt Testing and Validation

7.1 What is Prompt Testing and Validation?
7.2 The Importance of Testing and Validating Prompts
7.3 How to Perform Prompt Tests
7.4 Prompt Validation Techniques
7.5 Tools for Testing and Validating Prompts
7.6 Dealing with Inappropriate or Irrelevant Answers
7.7 Examples of Testing and Validating Prompts
7.8 Conclusion

Chapter 8: Advanced Applications of Prompt Engineering

8.1 Prompt Engineering for Creative Content Generation
8.2 Prompts for Data Analysis and Reporting
8.3 Prompts for Process Automation
8.4 Creating Prompts for Custom Model Training
8.5 Advanced Prompt Engineering Examples
8.6 Conclusion

Chapter 9: Advanced Prompt Engineering Applications

9.1 Sentiment Analysis with Prompts
9.2 Creative Text Generation with Prompts
9.3 Process Automation with Prompts
9.4 Data Search and Retrieval with Prompts
9.5 Developmental Conversational Applications with Prompts
9.6 Challenges in Advanced Prompt Applications
9.7 Conclusion

Chapter 10: Continuous Improvement and Experimentation in Prompt Engineering

10.1 The Importance of Continuous Improvement
10.2 Experimentation: The Process of Testing and Tuning
10.3 The Role of Feedback in Improving Prompts
10.4 A/B Testing Techniques in Prompts
10.5 Tools for Measuring Prompt Performance
10.6 Challenges in the Continuous Improvement Process
10.7 Conclusion

Chapter 11: Ethics and Responsibility in Prompt Engineering

11.1 The Importance of Ethics in Prompt Engineering
11.2 Identifying and Avoiding Bias in Prompts
11.3 Transparency and Clarity in Instructions
11.4 Prompts and Data Privacy
11.5 Social Responsibility in Prompt Creation
11.6 Ethical Challenges in Prompt Engineering
11.7 Conclusion

Chapter 12: Automation and Scalability in Prompt Engineering

12.1 The Need for Automation and Scalability
12.2 Prompt Automation Techniques
12.3 Scalability in Prompt Creation
12.4 Tools for Automation and Scalability
12.5 Automation and Scalability Application Examples
12.6 Challenges in Automation and Scalability
12.7 Conclusion

Chapter 13: The Future of Prompt Engineering: Trends and Innovations

13.1 The Evolution of Artificial Intelligence and Its Impact on Prompts
13.2 Contextual and Dynamic Prompts: The New Frontier
13.3 The Use of Multimodality for More Efficient Prompt Engineering
13.4 Autonomous Prompt Engineering: AI Creating Its Own Prompts
13.5 Mass Personalization with AI: Creating Unique Experiences for Each User
13.7 Conclusion
13.6 Challenges and Ethical Considerations in the Future of Prompt Engineering

Chapter 14: The Practice of Prompt Engineering: How to Create Effective Prompts and Optimize Interaction with AI

14.1 What is an Effective Prompt?
14.2 How to Structure Prompts for Maximum Clarity and Accuracy
14.3 Using Examples and Comparisons to Improve Prompts
14.4 Testing and Refining Prompts: The Importance of Feedback
14.5 Common Challenges in Creating Prompts and How to Overcome Them
14.6 The Importance of Continuous Experimentation in Prompt Engineering
14.7 Conclusion

Chapter 15: The Ethics of Prompt Engineering: Ensuring Responsible and Unbiased Responses

15.1 The Ethics of Artificial Intelligence
15.2 Avoiding Bias and Discrimination in Prompts
15.3 Ensuring Privacy and Confidentiality in AI Interactions
15.4 Avoiding the Generation of Harmful or Dangerous Content
15.5 How to Handle Sensitive Data and Critical Information
15.6 Responsibility when Creating Prompts for Generative AI
15.7 Best Practices for Ethical Prompts
15.8 Examples of Ethical and Unethical Prompts
15.9 Conclusion

Chapter 16: How to Optimize and Adjust Prompts for Consistent Results

16.1 What is Prompt Optimization?
16.2 The Importance of Being Specific in Prompts
16.3 Parameter Adjustment to Improve Results
16.4 Refining Prompts for Complex Topics
16.5 Using Examples to Guide the Answer
16.6 Testing and Iterating to Improve Results
16.7 Adjusting Complexity for Different Levels of Knowledge
16.8 The Impact of Prompt Formatting on Results
16.9 Final Thoughts on Prompt Optimization

Chapter 17: How to Evaluate and Measure the Quality of AI Responses

17.1 What is Quality Assessment of AI Responses?
17.2 Common Metrics for Evaluating Responses
17.3 How to Use Human Feedback to Evaluate Responses
17.4 AI Response Review Techniques
17.5 Tools for Measuring the Quality of Responses
17.6 Improving Prompts Based on Assessment
17.7 Final Thoughts on AI Response Evaluation

Chapter 18: How to Use Prompt Engineering for Specific AI Applications

18.1 What Are Specific Applications of AI?
18.2 Prompt Engineering for Text Generation
18.3 Engineering Prompts for Data Analysis
18.4 Engineering Prompts for Virtual Assistants
18.5 Process Automation Prompt Engineering
18.6 Final Thoughts on Specific Applications of AI

Chapter 19: How to Iterate and Improve Your Prompts Over Time

19.1 What is Prompt Iteration?
19.2 When to iterate your prompts?
19.3 Strategies for Prompt Iteration
19.4 Analyzing and Learning from AI Responses
19.5 Tools to Help with Prompt Iteration
19.6 A/B Testing of Prompts
19.7 Final Thoughts on Prompt Iteration

Chapter 20: Best Practices for Ensuring Ethical and Responsible AI Responses

20.1 What Are Ethical and Responsible AI Responses?
20.2 Importance of Considering Ethics When Creating Prompts
20.3 Strategies for Creating Ethical Prompts
20.4 How to Monitor and Adjust the Responses Generated
20.5 Implementation of Security Filters and Guidelines
20.6 Bias in AI and How to Mitigate Them
20.7 Final Thoughts on Ethical AI Responses

Chapter 21: The Evolution of AI Models and Their Implications for the Future of Prompt Engineering

21.1 The Evolution of AI Models: From Simple Rules to Complex Neural Networks
21.2 The Impact of Deep Learning on Prompt Engineering
21.3 Multimodal AI Models: Integration of Text, Image, and Audio
21.4 Customizing AI Models: More Specific and Contextual Prompts
21.5 The Need to Adapt Prompts for Different Types of AI
21.6 Future Trends in Prompt Engineering
21.7 Ethical and Social Implications of the Evolution of AI Models
21.8 Final Considerations

3. References

Chapter 1: Fundamentals of Prompt Engineering

In this chapter, we will explore the fundamental concepts of prompt engineering, providing a solid foundation for creating effective interactions with AI models. By understanding what prompts are and how they work, you'll be better prepared to use AI effectively and get the results you want.

1.1 What are Prompts?

- **Basic Definition**: A *prompt* is an input provided to an AI model, such as a question, command, or request, for the model to generate a response or perform a specific action. In other words, the prompt is the "question" or "instruction" given to the AI to produce a "result."

- **Practical Example**:
    - **Prompt**: "Explain the concept of supervised learning in artificial intelligence."
    - **Expected Answer**: The AI model should provide a clear and concise explanation of supervised learning, addressing its core components such as labeled data and classification algorithms.

- **Importance of the Prompt**: The way the prompt is worded has a major impact on the quality and relevance of the AI-generated response. Clear and well-structured prompts help ensure that the model correctly understands the task and generates the most appropriate response.

1.2 Difference Between Prompts and Queries

While both terms refer to requests made to a system, there is an important distinction between *prompts* and *queries*.

- **Queries**: Typically used in database systems or search engines, these are specific requests that aim to obtain concrete information or data. They usually have a well-defined format and expect an objective response.
    - **Sample Query**: "What is the capital of France?"

- o **Expected Answer**: "Paris"
- **Prompts**: These are more flexible and broad, often requiring a more elaborate, creative, or interpretive response. They are common in language models like GPT, where the goal can be to generate a text, solve a problem, or accomplish a creative task.
    - o **Sample Prompt**: "Describe the impact of the Industrial Revolution on European cities."
    - o **Expected Answer**: The AI model would provide a detailed explanation of the economic, social, and urban changes caused by the Industrial Revolution.
- **Key Difference**: Queries seek objective and direct data, while prompts aim to generate a more extensive response, with more context and details.

1.3 How Does AI Process Prompts?

To understand how an AI model responds to a prompt, it is essential to comprehend how it processes and interprets the input provided.

1. **Input Preprocessing**: When a prompt is received, the AI model first performs preprocessing of the text. This usually involves *tokenization*, which is the process of breaking up text into smaller units, called *tokens* (usually words or subwords). The model uses these units to understand the structure and meaning of the text.
    - o **Example**: If the prompt is "Explain what supervised learning is", the model can split the sentence into tokens such as: ["Explain", "the", "that", "is", "learning", "supervised"].
2. **Processing by the Language Model**: The AI model, such as GPT, uses neural networks trained on large amounts of text to identify patterns and relationships between tokens. It generates a response based on your training, considering the context of the prompt.

3. **Response Generation**: After processing the prompt, the model generates a sequence of words (response) based on the probabilities of which words come next. This sequence is adjusted to be grammatically correct and coherent with the context of the prompt.

    - **Practical Example of Processing**:
        - **Prompt**: "Talk about the history of artificial intelligence."
        - **Processing**: The model breaks the prompt into tokens, identifies context about "history" and "artificial intelligence," and generates a response that describes the origins of AI, from early concepts to current advancements.

1.4 Types of Language Models and Their Capabilities

Language models, such as GPT, have different capabilities, depending on how they have been trained and the type of task they can perform. Here are some common types of language models:

- **Generative Templates**: These templates are capable of generating text from any prompt. They produce creative and cohesive responses, making them ideal for tasks such as writing articles, generating code, or even composing literature.
    - **Example Generative Model Prompt**: "Write a poem about winter."
    - **Expected Answer**: A creative and original poem that describes typical winter scenes, using metaphors and other literary devices.
- **Command and Control Models**: Models such as virtual assistants (e.g., Siri, Alexa) are designed to perform specific actions, such as controlling devices, answering factual questions, or executing software commands.
    - **Example Virtual Assistant Prompt**: "Turn on the lights in the room."

- - **Expected Answer**: The virtual assistant performs the action of turning on the lights.
- **Multimodal Templates**: Templates like CLIP or DALL-E have the ability to process and generate both text and images. They are useful in tasks where the AI needs to understand and respond based on multimodal inputs (e.g., text and image).
  - **Example Prompt for Multimodal Model**: "Create an image of a cat wearing sunglasses."
  - **Expected Answer**: The model generates an image of a cat with sunglasses.

1.5 How Does the Prompt Formulation Impact the Response?

The way the prompt is worded has a direct impact on the quality and accuracy of the AI-generated response. Some tips for effective formulation include:

- **Be Clear and Specific**: Avoid ambiguity. The more specific the prompt, the more relevant the answer will be. For example, instead of asking "Talk about AI," ask "Explain how artificial intelligence can be applied in medicine for early diagnosis of diseases."

- **Provide Context**: When necessary, include relevant context to guide the AI in the response. This is especially important for creative or analytical tasks.
  - **Clear Prompt Example**: "Write an article about how AI is transforming the healthcare industry, with a focus on personalizing the treatment of cancer patients."

This chapter provides a solid foundation on what prompts are, how they are processed by AI models, and how you can create effective prompts to get accurate and relevant responses.

Chapter 2: Structure of an Efficient Prompt

In this chapter, we'll cover how to build an effective and efficient prompt. Prompt wording is crucial to ensure that the AI model correctly understands what you want and generates a useful and relevant response. Let's explore the essential elements that make up a well-structured prompt and how you can utilize them for better results.

2.1 Essential Elements of a Prompt

An effective prompt is not just a simple instruction. It should be clear, concise, and provide the proper context for the AI to generate the desired response. Here are the key elements you should consider when building a prompt:

1. **Clarity**: The prompt should be straightforward and easy to understand. Avoid ambiguous terms or vague instructions, as this can lead to irrelevant or inaccurate answers.

    - **Clear Prompt Example**: "Describe the benefits of solar energy for the environment."
    - **Example of an Ambiguous Prompt**: "Talk about energy."

2. **Context**: When necessary, provide background information to ensure that the AI understands the situation or the focus of the prompt.

    - **Example with Context**: "Explain how solar energy can help reduce dependence on fossil fuels and combat climate change."
    - **Example without Context**: "Explain how solar energy helps."

3. **Clear Objective**: Specify what you expect from AI. This helps direct the response to a specific format or content.

    - **Example with a Clear Objective**: "Write a 300-word summary of the environmental impacts of solar energy."
    - **Example without a clear purpose**: "Talk about solar energy."

4. **Proper Detailing**: Make sure to include enough details, but without overwhelming the prompt. The amount of detail can vary depending on the type of answer you want (short, long, technical, creative, etc.).
    - **Detailed Example**: "Write a comparison between solar and wind power, highlighting the pros and cons of each in the context of sustainability."
    - **Example Without Details**: "Compare solar and wind power."

2.2 How to Formulate a Clear and Objective Prompt

A well-formulated prompt guides the AI model precisely, helping to generate a relevant response. Here are some tips for creating clear and objective prompts:

1. **Use simple, straightforward language**: Avoid unnecessary jargon or overly technical terms unless it's relevant to the task.
    - **Example**: "Explain the importance of plastic recycling to reduce pollution."
    - **Mistake**: "Explain the relevance of synthetic polymers in reducing environmental pollution."

2. **Set the answer format**: If you need a specific answer (summary, list, explanation), ask for it directly.
    - **Sample Prompt with Defined Format**: "List 5 mental health benefits of meditation."
    - **Example of a Vague Prompt**: "Talk about the benefits of meditation."

3. **Be concise**: While details are important, avoid making the prompt excessively long. The AI model can become overwhelmed with irrelevant information.
    - **Concise Example**: "Explain Darwin's theory of evolution in 150 words."

- **Excessively Long Example**: "Explain in detail Darwin's theory of evolution, including all of its main concepts and how it has influenced modern biology, in up to 500 words."

2.3 Specifying Contexts and Details

Adding context and detail to your prompt is key to ensuring that the AI understands exactly what you want. This is especially important for tasks that require prior knowledge or a specific perspective.

1. **Provide relevant context**: If you're asking for an answer on a technical or specific topic, include background information that helps the model contextualize your answer.
    - **Example Prompt with Context**: "Explain the concept of deep learning in the context of artificial neural networks, mentioning the difference between shallow and deep neural networks."
    - **Example of a Prompt Without Context**: "Explain deep learning."
2. **Details about the target audience or tone**: If you want a response that is targeted at a specific audience or with a specific tone, include this information in the prompt.
    - **Example Prompt with Defined Tone**: "Write a white paper on cybersecurity, aimed at IT professionals."
    - **Example of a Prompt with no Defined Tone**: "Write about cybersecurity."

2.4 Practical Examples of Basic Prompts

Here are some examples of how to turn basic prompts into more effective prompts using the elements discussed:

1. **Example 1:**
    - **Basic Prompt**: "Talk about neural networks."

- **Efficient Prompt**: "Explain what artificial neural networks are and how they are used in image recognition tasks."

2. **Example 2:**
   - **Basic Prompt**: "Talk about global warming."
   - **Efficient Prompt**: "Describe the main causes of global warming and its impacts on marine ecosystems, including recent examples."

3. **Example 3:**
   - **Basic Prompt**: "How is the software developed?"
   - **Efficient Prompt**: "Explain the software development lifecycle, including the requirements analysis, design, implementation, testing, and maintenance phases."

2.5 How to Improve the Quality of Prompts with Iteration

Creating a good prompt often involves an iterative process. You can start with a simple prompt and refine it as you test the AI's response, tweaking details to improve the quality of the interaction.

1. **First Version of the Prompt**:
   - **Initial Prompt**: "Talk about the importance of financial planning."
   - **Initial Answer**: It can be vague or generic.

2. **Prompt Refinement**:
   - **Refined Prompt**: "Explain the importance of personal financial planning for long-term security, including practical tips on how to get started."
   - **Expected Response**: AI generates a more focused and useful response, with practical tips.

3. **Additional Adjustments**: Continue to refine the prompt to make the response even more accurate and useful if necessary.

This chapter has highlighted the importance of building clear, concise, and well-contextualized prompts. By following these guidelines, you can significantly improve the quality of AI-generated responses, making the interaction more effective and targeted to what you really need.

Chapter 3: Types of Prompts and Their Applications

In this chapter, we'll explore the different types of prompts you can use when interacting with AI models. Each type of prompt has a specific application, depending on what you want to achieve with the template. Let's look at the most common types of prompts, such as open-ended questions, closed-ended questions, action prompts, and creative prompts, as well as their best practices and examples.

3.1 Question Prompts

Definition: Question prompts are used when you want to get a straightforward and objective answer from the AI. This type of prompt can be either a simple question or a more elaborate one, depending on the complexity of the answer you want.

- **Example of a Closed Question**: "What is the capital of France?"
    - **Expected Answer**: "Paris"
    - *Explanation*: This is an example of a closed question, where the answer is objective and specific.
- **Open-ended Question Example**: "What are the main challenges facing business leaders in the current scenario?"
    - **Expected Response**: The model can list challenges such as technological innovation, team management, sustainability, among others.
    - *Explanation*: Here, the model offers a broader, more interpretive response, based on its understanding of the context.

Applications: This type of prompt is ideal for obtaining objective information or for stimulating the AI to provide detailed explanations on a specific topic.

3.2 Instruction Prompts

Definition: Instruction prompts are used when you want the AI to perform a specific action or provide a response in a given format. Instruction can be a simple or complex task, and the AI model is directed to follow these steps or formats in a clear manner.

- **Simple Instruction Example**: "List the steps to create a website using WordPress."
    - **Expected Answer**: The template generates a list with the basic steps, such as choosing a domain, hosting the website, installing WordPress, choosing a theme, etc.
- **Example of Complex Instruction**: "Create a 300-word summary of the history of the Roman Empire, highlighting major events and historical figures."
    - **Expected Answer**: The template generates a concise summary, covering key historical landmarks and figures such as Julius Caesar and Augustus.

Applications: Statement prompts are ideal for when you want the model to perform a structured task or provide an answer in a specific format, such as a list, summary, or analysis.

3.3 Creative Stimulus Prompts

Definition: These prompts are intended to stimulate the model's creativity by making it generate original or creative content. They are used for activities such as creative writing, idea generation, or any type of work that requires out-of-the-box thinking.

- **Creative Prompt Example**: "Write a poem about spring, using metaphors and personification."
    - **Expected Answer**: The model generates a poem with creative elements, using metaphors such as "the wind danced in the trees" and personification by saying "spring smiled on the field".

- **Example of a Creative Prompt in Storytelling**: "Create a short story about a robot that discovers the meaning of friendship."
    - **Expected Answer**: The model creates a fictional story, with characters and plot, exploring friendship in a creative way.

Applications: Creative prompts are great for activities such as writing fiction, creating ideas for projects, crafting stories, or even creating artistic content such as music and poetry.

3.4 Analysis or Explanation Prompts

Definition: These prompts are used when you want the AI to provide a detailed analysis or explanation on a particular topic. The model should explain, compare, or analyze information, evidence, or situations based on its prior knowledge.

- **Example of Analysis Prompt**: "Analyze the impacts of the Industrial Revolution on European society in the nineteenth century."
    - **Expected Answer**: The model provides a detailed analysis, addressing how the Industrial Revolution affected the economy, working conditions, and social relations.
- **Example Explanation Prompt**: "Explain the difference between supervised learning and unsupervised learning."
    - **Expected Answer**: The model describes the characteristics of the two types of learning, such as the use of labeled data in the supervised and the search for patterns in the unsupervised.

Applications: These prompts are useful when you need the AI to provide a clear explanation, analyze a situation, or make a comparison between two or more concepts.

3.5 Persuasion or Argumentation Prompts

Definition: Persuasion or argumentation prompts are used when you want the AI to build a solid argument, defend an idea, or convince someone of a point of view. This type of prompt requires the template to provide a rationale or reasons that support a position.

- **Example of Persuasion Prompt**: "Defend the importance of distance education in the modern world, considering technological advances and accessibility."
    - **Expected Answer**: The model makes a case for distance education, including points about flexibility, affordability, and technological advancements that facilitate remote learning.
- **Example Pitch Prompt**: "Argue against the idea that self-driving cars can be a safe solution to urban traffic."
    - **Expected Response**: The model provides an argument, highlighting potential challenges such as technological failures, ethical issues, and the impact on employment.

Applications: These prompts are useful for generating persuasive debates, discussions, or speeches. They can be used in academic contexts, political contexts, or in any situation where it is necessary to defend a point of view.

3.6 Comparison Prompts

Definition: Comparison prompts ask the model to compare two or more elements, highlighting similarities and differences. These prompts are useful when you want to understand how two concepts, products, events, or situations compare to each other.

- **Simple Comparison Prompt Example**: "Compare solar and wind power in terms of cost and efficiency."
    - **Expected Answer**: The model compares the installation and operating costs of the two energy sources and their efficiencies in different contexts, such as regions with different climates.
- **Example of a Complex Comparison Prompt**: "Compare the economic and social impacts of the French Revolution and the Industrial Revolution."

- **Expected Answer**: The model addresses the similarities and differences in the economic, social, and political changes caused by each revolution.

Applications: These prompts are ideal for when you want to understand the differences and similarities between concepts, events, products, or ideas. They help clarify how elements interrelate.

3.7 How to Choose the Right Prompt Type?

The choice of prompt type depends on the purpose of the interaction with the AI. To decide which type to use, consider:

1. **What is the purpose of the answer?** If you need an objective answer, a closed-ended question may be suitable. If the task requires creativity, use a creative prompt.

2. **What is the level of detail required?** Whether you need an in-depth analysis or a detailed explanation, opt for analysis prompts.

3. **What answer format do you want?** If you need a list or a summary, use how-to prompts.

This chapter has explained the different types of prompts and their applications, offering practical examples to help you choose the right prompt type for your needs. By understanding the types of prompts and how to apply them correctly, you can maximize the effectiveness of interacting with AI models and achieve better results.

Chapter 4: Advanced Prompt Engineering Techniques

This chapter explores advanced techniques for refining and optimizing your prompts, allowing you to achieve more accurate, creative, and useful results. We'll dive deeper into prompt enhancement methods such as using contexts and examples, breaking down complex tasks, and approaches like prompt chaining and few-shot learning. Applying these techniques can transform basic interactions with AI models into highly relevant and targeted responses.

4.1 Use of Contexts and Examples

Definition: Including context and examples in your prompt is an advanced technique that helps the model better understand the task by providing a more solid foundation for the response. The context can be an additional explanation of the problem or a description of the desired format for the response. The examples provide the model with a direct reference about the style or structure of the expected response.

- **Example Prompt with Context and Examples**:
    - **Context**: "You are an expert in financial education and will explain the concept of household budgeting."
    - **Prompt**: "Explain what a household budget is, providing examples of spending categories and strategies for tracking expenses."
    - **Expected Example**: The model generates a structured response, with spending categories (housing, food, leisure, etc.) and control strategies (such as the use of spreadsheets or budgeting apps).
- **Example with Context and Style Examples**:
    - **Context**: "You're a science fiction writer, and you're creating a new universe for a story."

- **Example**: "The planet Gorthus is a land of incessant storms and luminescent vegetation. Write a brief description of how the inhabitants interact with the environment."
- **Expected Answer**: The model generates a detailed description of the environment and the inhabitants' interactions with it, using a narrative style characteristic of science fiction.

Applications: Using context and examples is particularly useful when you want a specific style or tone, or when the task requires the model to understand a complex scenario or set of information.

4.2 Chunking

Definition: Chunking is the technique of breaking down a broad request into several smaller, manageable chunks. This helps the AI focus on one task at a time, increasing the accuracy and clarity of the final answer.

- **Example of Prompt Chunking**:
    - **Complex Task**: "Explain how to create a complete mobile app, including planning, design, development, and release."
    - **Division of Task**:
        1. "First, describe the planning required to create a mobile app."
        2. "Next, explain the key aspects of designing a mobile app."
        3. "Then, talk about the process of developing a mobile app."
        4. "Finally, explain the steps required to launch a mobile app."
    - **Expected Response**: The template will answer each part of the task separately, giving you a detailed and organized view of each step of the process.

Applications: This technique is useful for issues that involve multiple aspects or steps, such as step-by-step guides, complex tutorials, or tasks that require analysis at different levels.

4.3 Prompt Chaining

Definition: Prompt chaining involves the use of a sequence of interlocking prompts. Instead of asking for a single answer to a complex task, you break down the process into a series of iterations. Each new interaction depends on the previous response, allowing the AI to refine its responses based on the information provided along the chain.

- **Prompt Chaining Example**:
    - **First Prompt**: "Describe the major events of the French Revolution."
    - **Expected Answer**: The template lists the key events, such as the Fall of the Bastille, the execution of Louis XVI, etc.
    - **According to Prompt**: "How did these events affect France's politics and economy at the time?"
    - **Expected Answer**: The model does an analysis of political and economic transformation, referencing the events mentioned in the first prompt.

Applications: Prompt chaining is ideal for topics or tasks that require gradual development of information, such as solving complex problems or in-depth analysis of a topic.

4.4 Few-Shot Learning

Definition: Few-shot learning is a technique that allows you to train an AI model with a small number of examples, rather than a large volume of data. By using this technique, you provide some examples of how the task should be performed, and the model uses these examples to generate more accurate responses, even with limited information.

- **Example of Few-Shot Learning**:
    - **Task**: "Classify the following passages of text as 'positive' or 'negative.'"
    - **Example 1**: "This product exceeded all my expectations!" → **Positive**
    - **Example 2**: "Delivery was delayed and service was not good." → **Negative**
    - **Prompt**: "Now rate the following comment: 'The quality of service is excellent, but the delivery took a while.'"
    - **Expected Response**: "Positive"
    - *Explanation*: Even with just two examples, the model can learn to correctly classify other pieces of text.

Applications: Few-shot learning is useful when you don't have a large amount of data or examples, but still need the model to perform tasks accurately. It's a powerful technique when applied correctly, especially in text classification or analysis tasks.

4.5 Using Metadata for Response Refinement

Definition: Meta information refers to adding extra information to your prompt to further refine the response you want from the AI. This can include instructions on the style, tone, target audience, or other aspects of the content generated.

- **Example of a Prompt with Metainformation**:
    - **Prompt**: "Explain the concept of machine learning simply, as if you were explaining it to a 10-year-old."
    - **Expected Answer**: The model uses an accessible and simplified tone, explaining machine learning as a process in which "the computer learns from examples, just as you learn to ride a bike by watching others do it."

- **Example of a Prompt with Style Metainformation**:
    - **Prompt**: "Write an article on artificial intelligence with a formal and technical tone, suitable for an academic audience."
    - **Expected Answer**: The model generates a more technical text, with area-specific vocabulary and a more formal structure.

Applications: Using metadata is particularly useful when you need the AI to communicate in a specific way, whether it's adapting the tone or style to suit the audience or format required.

4.6 Practical Examples of Advanced Techniques

1. **Technique: Use of Context and Examples**
    - **Prompt**: "Explain Einstein's theory of relativity in a way that is accessible to a lay audience, using a simple analogy."
    - **Expected Answer**: The model creates an explanation using an accessible analogy, such as comparing spacetime to a stretched sheet of rubber.

2. **Technique: Chunking (Division of Complex Tasks)**
    - **Prompt**: "Explain how to build a website: 1) plan the layout, 2) choose a platform, 3) define the content."
    - **Expected Response**: The template answers each step separately, detailing the planning, platform choice, and content creation.

3. **Technique: Prompt Chaining**
    - **Prompt**: "What are the causes of World War I?" (Reply)
    - **Following up with**: "How did these causes lead to the involvement of the major European powers?"
    - **Expected Answer**: The model gradually expands the explanation, taking into account the causes and their effects.

4.7 Conclusion

Advanced prompt engineering techniques allow for greater control over the responses generated by AI models by improving the relevance, clarity, and depth of the content. By understanding and applying these techniques, you'll be able to optimize your interactions with AI and achieve your goals more effectively.

With mastery of these strategies, you'll be well-equipped to tackle more complex tasks, extract deeper insights, and get more accurate and relevant answers.

This chapter explained the advanced techniques for optimizing and refining prompts. By implementing these strategies, you can significantly improve the quality of AI-generated responses by achieving more effective and personalized results.

Chapter 5: Common Challenges and How to Overcome Them in Prompt Engineering

In this chapter, we will explore the key challenges faced in prompt engineering when interacting with AI models. Understanding these obstacles is essential so that you can overcome them effectively and improve the accuracy and relevance of the responses you get from AI. We will also discuss best practices and techniques for mitigating these issues.

5.1 Ambiguity in Prompts

Definition: Ambiguity occurs when a prompt is not clear enough, leading to multiple interpretations or inaccurate results. This can happen due to the use of vague terms, lack of context, or the absence of essential information.

- **Example of an Ambiguous Prompt**: "Talk about the market."
    - **Problem**: AI may not know if you are referring to the financial market, labor market, consumer market, or other type of market.
    - **Expected Result**: Vague or disjointed response, which does not meet your specific need.
- **How to Overcome**: Be as specific as possible in your prompt, providing additional context when needed.
    - **Clear Prompt Example**: "Talk about the current financial market, covering the main investment trends in 2024."
        - **Expected Outcome**: AI offers a focused response to financial market trends, such as investments in stocks and cryptocurrencies.

Applications: Avoiding ambiguity is crucial when you want AI to provide detailed and targeted information. The clearer and more specific your prompt is, the better the answer.

5.2 Model Knowledge Limitations

Definition: AI models have limits on their knowledge, especially regarding up-to-date events and data. This can result in inaccurate or outdated answers, particularly on topics that involve new or very specific information.

- **Knowledge-Limiting Prompt Example**: "What is the latest release of the 2024 Tesla model?"
    - **Problem**: The AI may not have access to updated information in real time, especially after its training date. It may provide outdated or incorrect information.
- **How to Overcome**: Recognize that AI models may not have the latest information, and when necessary, consult with external sources to supplement the response.
    - **Example of Prompt with Recognized Limitation**: "What were the electric car trends through 2023, and what innovations were expected for the future?"
        - **Expected Outcome**: AI provides an analysis of trends and innovations through 2023, based on its knowledge.

Applications: This challenge is especially important in rapidly changing areas, such as technology, science, or politics. Be sure to adjust the prompt according to the limitations of the model.

5.3 Superficial or Generic Answers

Definition: When an AI model responds superficially or generically, it can be caused by prompts that do not provide enough information or context to generate a deep or detailed response.

- **Generic Prompt Example**: "Explain the impact of social media."
    - **Problem**: AI can give a very broad and superficial answer, such as: "Social networks have a great impact on society."
    - **Expected Outcome**: Vague answer with no details or nuances.

- **How to Overcome**: P for more in-depth answers, provide additional information, define a clear scope, and, if necessary, request examples or analysis.

    - **Clear and Detailed Prompt Example**: "Explain the impact of social media on consumers' buying behavior, highlighting key changes over the past five years."

        - **Expected Outcome**: AI offers a more focused analysis, detailing how social media influences purchasing decisions, with examples of marketing strategies and behavior changes.

Applications: When you need a more detailed or specific answer, it's important to steer the AI towards a narrower theme or perspective, avoiding broad and vague topics.

5.4 Complex or Ambiguous Sentences

Definition: Using complex or ambiguous sentences in your prompt can make it difficult for the AI to understand, resulting in inaccurate responses. This is especially important in tasks that require a clear interpretation of your request.

- **Example of a Complex and Ambiguous Sentence**: "Dissertation on the main concepts of psychology that influence consumption decisions, without forgetting the theories on social and emotional behavior, considering the economic and cultural implications."

    - **Problem**: The AI can feel overwhelmed and provide a confusing or unfocused response.

- **How to Overshoot**: Simplify the structure of your prompt and break it down into smaller, more manageable chunks.

    - **Simplified Prompt Example**: "Talk about how psychological theories influence consumer decisions. Then explain how social and emotional behavior affects consumer choices."

- **Expected Outcome**: AI handles the separate parts and provides more focused and clear answers.

Applications: When dealing with complex topics, it is essential to use clear and concise sentences, breaking down questions into easy-to-cover segments.

5.5 Tendency to Predictable or Common Responses

Definition: AI models often generate predictable or common responses, especially if the prompt is generic or if the AI has been trained with widely available data. This can lead to responses that don't add significant value or new perspectives.

- **Example of Predictable Prompt**: "Talk about the benefits of meditation."
    - **Problem**: AI can generate a predictable response, such as, "Meditation helps reduce stress and improves mental health."
    - **Expected Outcome**: A response that does not present new information or deep insights.
- **How to Overcome**:P To avoid common answers, ask more specific questions or ask for a more in-depth analysis, based on specific research or cases.
    - **Specific Prompt Example**: "Explain how meditation can affect neuroscience, including recent studies on the effects on the brain and the reduction of chronic stress."
        - **Expected Outcome**: AI provides a more detailed answer, with reference to scientific studies and specific information.

Applications: This challenge is overcome by refining your prompt to explore lesser-covered areas or asking for deeper, more personalized analytics.

5.6 How to Overcome Common Challenges: Tips and Best Practices

1. **Specific**: The more details you provide in your prompt, the more likely you are to get an accurate answer. Avoid generalizations and offer context when necessary.

2. **Test and Adjust**: If the answer is not satisfactory, adjust the prompt and try again. Interacting with AI models can require trial and error.

3. **Break Down Complex Tasks**: If the subject is complex, break it down into smaller parts and provide clear steps for the AI to follow.

4. **Use Examples**: Provide clear examples of how you want the answer to be structured. This helps the AI understand the task better.

5. **Consider Knowledge Limitations**: Keep in mind that AI models may not have up-to-date information. When necessary, provide temporal information at the prompt to adjust expectations.

6. **Simplify Language**: Avoid complex sentences and simplify your request so that the AI can easily understand.

5.7 Conclusion

Understanding and overcoming common challenges in prompt engineering is essential to getting the best possible answers from an AI model. By applying the techniques and best practices discussed in this chapter, you will be able to avoid ambiguous, superficial, or inaccurate answers, and achieve more effective and relevant results. The key to improving interactions with AI is to constantly refine prompts, considering the limitations of the model and adjusting your prompts as needed.

This chapter covered the key challenges encountered in prompt engineering, offering solutions and examples to overcome them. By applying these strategies, you will be able to enhance your interactions with AI, resulting in more accurate, creative, and useful responses.

Chapter 6: Optimizing Prompts to Maximize Results

In this chapter, we will explore how to optimize prompts for the best possible results when interacting with artificial intelligence systems. Prompt optimization is an essential skill for maximizing the accuracy, relevance, and creativity of AI responses. We will discuss techniques to improve the effectiveness of prompts by avoiding generic responses and ensuring that AI provides more accurate and detailed responses.

6.1 What is Prompt Optimization?

Definition: Prompt optimization is the process of adjusting and improving the instructions given to the AI to achieve the desired results with greater accuracy and relevance. This involves carefully choosing words and structuring prompts in a way that guides the AI more efficiently.

- **Objective**: To ensure that the AI model clearly understands what is expected of it and that the responses are tailored to the user's context and need.

6.2 Techniques to Optimize Prompts

Here are some key techniques you can use to optimize your prompts:

- **Be Specific and Clear**: The more specific your prompt is, the more detailed the AI's response will be. Clarity is key to avoiding vague or out-of-context answers.
    - **Practical Example:**
        - **Generic Prompt**: "Talk about AI."
        - **Optimized Prompt**: "Explain how artificial intelligence can be used in the healthcare industry to improve the early diagnosis of diseases."

The optimized version provides clearer context, resulting in a more focused response.

- **Use Examples**: Including examples in your prompt helps the AI understand the format and style of the desired response.

    - **Practical Example**:
        - **Generic Prompt**: "Write a poem."
        - **Optimized Prompt**: "Write a William Wordsworth-style poem about the beauty of nature, including the image of a mountain and the sound of a stream."

The example given allows the AI to better understand the desired style and theme.

- **Limit the Scope**: By clearly defining the scope of the response, you can avoid answers that are too broad or irrelevant.

    - **Practical Example**:
        - **Generic Prompt**: "Explain the physics."
        - **Optimized Prompt**: "Explain the basic principles of quantum physics, with a focus on wave-particle duality."

The optimized prompt specifies the topic and limits the explanation, which results in a more accurate response.

- **Use Formatting and Structure**: Clear formatting can help the AI better understand what is expected in the response. If a specific format is required, include that information in the prompt.

    - **Practical Example**:
        - **Generic Prompt**: "Describe the types of intelligence."
        - **Optimized Prompt**: "List and briefly describe the 3 main types of intelligence according to Howard Gardner's theory of multiple intelligences: linguistic, logical-mathematical, and spatial."

Using a structured list makes it easier for the AI to understand the desired format.

6.3 Strategies for Obtaining High-Quality Results

- **Break Down Complex Tasks into Smaller Steps**: If the prompt involves a complex task, consider breaking the question into several parts. This makes it easier for AI to handle each aspect more efficiently.
    - **Practical Example:**
        - **Generic Prompt**: "Create a business plan."
        - **Optimized Prompt**: "Create a business plan for an AI startup. First, describe the company's mission and vision. Then, do a market analysis. Finally, provide a financial projection for the first 3 years."

Breaking down the task into clear steps allows for more organized and detailed answers.

- **Ask Direct Questions**: Open-ended questions can generate generic answers. Instead, formulate direct questions to guide the AI to provide more focused responses.
    - **Practical Example:**
        - **Generic Prompt**: "What do you know about the weather?"
        - **Optimized Prompt**: "What are the main factors that influence the climate of the Amazon region?"

The optimized version is more targeted and results in a more accurate and relevant response.

- **Ask for Justifications and Details:** If you need a more in-depth answer, ask the AI to justify or detail their answers. This increases the depth of interaction.

- **Practical Example**:
  - **Generic Prompt**: "What are the advantages of solar energy?"
  - **Optimized Prompt**: "What are the top 3 advantages of solar energy for environmental sustainability? Justify each of them with examples."

By asking for justifications, you get more detailed and well-reasoned answers.

6.4 Adjusting the Tone and Style of the Response

Prompt optimization doesn't just refer to the content of the response, but also to the tone and style. You can adjust the tone of the AI so that it produces formal, informal, persuasive, or technical responses, depending on your goal.

- **Practical Example**:
  - **Generic Prompt**: "Explain what machine learning is."
  - **Optimized Prompt (formal):** "Provide a technical explanation of the concept of machine learning, focusing on its key techniques and applications."
  - **Optimized Prompt (informal):** "Can you explain to me what machine learning is in a simple way, as if I were a beginner?"

Depending on the tone requested, the AI will adjust its response to be more technical or more accessible.

6.5 Common Mistakes When Creating Prompts and How to Avoid Them

- **Being Too Vague or Generic**: Generic prompts result in equally generic responses, which may not be helpful or accurate. Always try to be clear and specific.
  - **Example error**: "Talk about the future."

- **Correction**: "Explain how emerging technologies such as AI and blockchain could impact the global economy over the next 10 years."
- **Lack of Context**: If you don't provide adequate context, the AI may not understand the scenario and generate inappropriate responses.
  - **Example error**: "What are the advantages of technology?"
  - **Correction**: "What are the advantages of blockchain technology in the financial sector, especially in relation to security and transparency?"
- **Ambiguous Instructions**: Avoid using ambiguous words or phrases that can be interpreted in a variety of ways. Be clear on what you want.
  - **Example error**: "Talk about intelligence."
  - **Correction**: "Explain the top 3 theories about human intelligence and their implications for education."

6.6 Testing and Refining Prompts

Prompt optimization is an iterative process. After testing a prompt and getting a response, evaluate whether it meets your needs. Otherwise, refine the prompt until you reach the expected result. AI can provide different results from slight variations in prompts, so experimentation is a key to success.

- **Practical Example**:
  - **First Test**: "Explain the theory of relativity."
  - **Result**: Very vague and generic answer.
  - **Refinement**: "Explain Einstein's theory of relativity, with emphasis on the differences between special and general relativity."
  - **Expected Outcome**: A more detailed and accurate answer, addressing the specific concepts.

6.7 Conclusion

Prompt optimization is an essential skill for getting more effective and relevant results when working with AI. By being specific, using examples, structuring requests correctly, and adjusting the tone and style of the response, you can maximize the potential of AI in your interactions. In addition, constant practice and analysis of the results help to refine your prompts, making your interactions more efficient and accurate.

In this chapter, we cover the key strategies and techniques for optimizing your prompts. With these tools, you'll be able to achieve more accurate, creative, and relevant responses by applying prompt engineering in a variety of scenarios.

This chapter has provided a solid foundation for understanding the importance of prompt optimization and how to use it to maximize the effectiveness of your AI interactions.

Chapter 7: Prompt Testing and Validation

In the previous chapter, we covered how to optimize your prompts to maximize the results you get with AI. Now, let's explore the process of testing and validating these prompts, which is critical to ensuring that you're getting the answers you want. Testing and validation help identify what adjustments are needed to improve the accuracy, clarity, and relevance of the AI's responses.

7.1 What is Prompt Testing and Validation?

Definition: Prompt testing and validation refers to the process of evaluating the effectiveness of prompts created to ensure that they produce the desired results, accurately and relevantly. This process involves running a series of tests to evaluate the AI's response to different prompt variations.

- **Objective**: Validate that the prompts are actually delivering the type of response expected and make adjustments to improve the quality of the interaction with the AI.

7.2 The Importance of Testing and Validating Prompts

Before implementing a prompt into a real project or using it on a recurring basis, it's crucial to conduct tests to:

- **Check for Clarity**: Make sure the AI fully understands what is being ordered. A poorly structured prompt can generate inaccurate or irrelevant responses.

- **Evaluate the Quality of Responses**: Test whether the responses provided are sufficiently detailed, complete, and in the desired tone.

- **Adjust Accuracy**: Refine prompts to make responses more specific and aligned with the user's goals.

- **Reduce Ambiguity**: Identify and eliminate points of ambiguity in prompts, which can lead to misinterpretations.

7.3 How to Perform Prompt Tests

To perform effective testing, follow these steps:

1. **Define the Test Objectives**: The first step is to clearly understand what you expect from the test. The goal might be, for example, to check the accuracy, relevance, or depth of the answer.

    - **Example**: If your goal is to test clarity, your goal is to verify that the AI correctly understood the prompt and provided an answer that is in line with what was requested.

2. **Create Prompt Variations**: Test different versions of the same prompt. Variations can be made by changing words, adding details, or changing the format of the question.

    - **Practical Example**:
        - **Version 1**: "Explain the benefits of solar energy."
        - **Version 2**: "What are the top 5 benefits of solar energy for the environment?"
        - **Version 3**: "How can solar energy positively impact the environment, especially in reducing carbon emissions?"

3. **Run the Tests**: Use the prompt variations in your AI tool and collect the answers. Each version of the prompt must be tested separately.

4. **Evaluate Responses**: Analyze the responses you get to determine which version of the prompt generated the best results. Consider criteria such as clarity, depth, relevance, and tone.

    - **Practical Example**: If version 3 generated a more complete and detailed answer, while version 1 generated a very superficial answer, version 3 would be the most effective.

5. **Adjust and Refine Prompts**: Based on the results of the tests, refine your prompts to improve the quality of the answers. This may involve removing ambiguities or adding more details to the request.

7.4 Prompt Validation Techniques

Prompt validation is a critical part of the prompt engineering process. It ensures that the adjustments made to the prompts actually bring the desired results. Here are some effective validation techniques:

- **Iteration Validation**: Make adjustments to the prompts, test them, and validate them multiple times until you reach the optimal result. Continuous improvement is essential.
    - **Practical Example**: After testing the first prompt, you can identify an area that needs more context. Adjust the prompt and test again to see if the result improves.
- **Compliance Testing**: Validate that the responses are in line with the scope and parameters defined in the prompt. This helps ensure that the AI is delivering exactly what was ordered.
    - **Practical Example**: If you ask for a technical explanation of a scientific theory, make sure the AI is not providing a simplified or inaccurate explanation.
- **Validation with Real Use Case**: Simulate a real use case to verify that the prompt meets the needs of the end user. This helps validate whether interacting with AI is actually useful in a practical scenario.
    - **Practical Example**: If you're creating a prompt to be used in a customer service tool, simulate a real customer interacting with the AI to ensure that the prompt generates relevant and accurate responses.

7.5 Tools for Testing and Validating Prompts

Some tools can be very useful for testing and validating your prompts more efficiently. Here are some options:

- **ChatGPT (or other AI model):** One of the easiest and most accessible tools for testing prompts, as you can quickly test variations and get real-time responses.

- **AI platforms like OpenAI Playground, Hugging Face**: Tools like these allow you to interact with AI models in a controlled environment, making it easy to evaluate different responses.

- **Automated Testing**: In more advanced cases, you can create automated test scripts that send prompts to the AI and collect the answers in a systematic way, which can be useful for validating large amounts of data.

7.6 Dealing with Inappropriate or Irrelevant Answers

During tests, it is common for some answers to not meet your expectations. Here are some strategies to improve these results:

- **Adjust the Prompt Structure**: If the answer was vague or irrelevant, try reframing the prompt to be more direct or more specific.

    - **Practical Example**:
        - **Inappropriate Prompt**: "Talk about the technology."
        - **Irrelevant Answer**: "Technology involves multiple fields and constantly evolves."
        - **Adjusted Prompt**: "Explain the main types of technology used in mobile devices, with a focus on connectivity technologies and processors."

- **Review the Context**: If the AI has not provided the correct answer, review the context given in the prompt. Make sure that all the necessary details have been included so that the AI clearly understands what is being requested.

- **Use Follow-up Questions**: If the initial response is not satisfactory, provide more information or ask follow-up questions to clarify and obtain additional details.

    - **Practical Example**:
        - **Inadequate Answer**: "AI can be useful in many areas."

- **Follow-up**: "What are the main examples of AI use in the healthcare sector?"

7.7 Examples of Testing and Validating Prompts

- **Example 1**: **Prompt**: "Talk about the advantages of using AI in education."
    - **Test 1**: The model generates a very vague answer, saying only that AI can help in many areas.
    - **Fit**: "Explain how AI can be used to personalize the learning experience, focusing on specific examples of educational applications."
    - **Test 2**: The answer is more detailed and focuses on practical examples, such as intelligent tutoring systems.
- **Example 2**: **Prompt**: "Explain the fermentation process."
    - **Test 1**: The AI provides a general explanation of fermentation without details.
    - **Adjustment**: "Explain the process of alcoholic fermentation, mentioning the biochemical steps and the conditions necessary for it to occur."
    - **Test 2**: The answer becomes more specific, covering the detailed steps of alcoholic fermentation.

7.8 Conclusion

Prompt testing and validation are essential steps in the prompt engineering process to ensure that you get the best results from AI. The constant practice of testing variations, evaluating responses, and refining prompts helps maximize the effectiveness of interacting with AI models. With the methods and examples presented in this chapter, you'll be better prepared to create optimized prompts that meet your needs and expectations.

This chapter has detailed best practices for testing and validating prompts, providing a solid foundation for ensuring that you are always receiving the most accurate and relevant responses from AI.

Chapter 8: Advanced Applications of Prompt Engineering

In this chapter, we will explore some of the advanced applications of prompt engineering, covering how you can use this skill in different contexts and areas of expertise, obtaining more effective and personalized results. Through practical examples, we will explain how to structure prompts for specific cases, including content creation, automation, data analysis, and even training AI models.

8.1 Prompt Engineering for Creative Content Generation

Definition: Creative content generation involves utilizing AI to create text, images, music, or other types of media autonomously or with minimal supervision. Prompt engineering is essential to guide AI to produce high-quality, relevant content.

- **Practical Example of Creative Text Generation**: If you need the AI to write a story, you will need to provide details about the style, plot, characters, and tone. The more detailed and specific the prompt, the more relevant the content generated will be.
    - **Creative Prompt**: "Create a short sci-fi story set in 2150, where artificial intelligence controls every aspect of human life, but a group of scientists try to destroy the system. The protagonist is a young hacker who discovers a secret that could change the future of humanity."
    - **Expected Result**: The AI creates a complete narrative, with characters, plot, conflicts, and a coherent conclusion, respecting the requested style and details.

Applications:

- **Creation of Blogs and Articles**: Generation of blog posts on specific topics.
- **Video Scripts**: Creation of scripts for videos or films.

- **Advertising and Marketing**: Development of slogans, advertising campaigns, and promotional content.

8.2 Prompts for Data Analysis and Reporting

Definition: Data analysis involves extracting meaningful information from large volumes of data. Prompt engineering can be used to direct AI to identify patterns, generate reports, and extract valuable insights, based on numerical or textual data.

- **Practical Example of Data Analysis**: If you want the AI to analyze financial data and provide specific insights, the prompt needs to include what aspects or metrics you want to investigate.
    - **Analysis Prompt**: "Analyze the financial data of the technology sector from 2020 to 2023. Identify the top 3 growth trends and highlight the sectors with the highest increase in investment."
    - **Expected Outcome**: AI generates a detailed report, highlighting key growth sectors within the technology, such as artificial intelligence and cloud computing, based on investment data.

Applications:

- **Sales Analytics**: Identifying patterns in sales data to predict future trends.
- **Market Reports**: Generate reports on consumer trends and changes in market behavior.
- **Market Research**: Processing of collected data to generate in-depth insights and analysis.

8.3 Prompts for Process Automation

Definition: Process automation allows AI to perform repetitive or rule-based tasks, saving time and human effort. This includes automating business processes such as email generation, reporting, and customer service.

- **Practical Task Automation Example:** P automate the generation of responses to support emails, the prompt needs to clearly state the tone and information that the response should include.

    - **Email Response Automation Prompt**: "Generate a professional and polite response for a customer who has reached out due to a delay in order delivery. Apologize, offer a solution, and provide an estimated timeframe for the new delivery."

    - **Expected Outcome**: AI generates a cordial and well-structured response, addressing the customer's complaint effectively and professionally, offering a concrete solution.

Applications:

- **Customer Service**: Automatic responses to frequently asked questions or common issues.

- **Task and Project Management**: Generate reports and automatic updates on project progress.

- **Automation of Administrative Processes**: Automatic generation of documents, such as contracts or financial reports.

8.4 Creating Prompts for Custom Model Training

Definition: As you explore customizing AI models, you may need to train AI in a specific domain, such as the terminology of a technical area, consumer behavior, or even specific interaction patterns.

- **Practical Example of Custom Training**: If you want to train a model to understand industry-specific jargon, such as legal or medicine, you'll need to adapt the prompt to include this technical vocabulary.

    - **Model Training Prompt**: "Train the AI model to recognize and understand legal terms related to business contracts, such as exclusivity, non-compete, and contract termination clauses."

- **Expected Outcome**: AI learns to correctly interpret legal terms and concepts, and can offer more accurate and contextualized answers within that domain.

Applications:

- **Industry-Specific Virtual Assistants**: AI training for industries such as healthcare, education, and law.
- **Sentiment Analysis in Specific Texts**: Training models to detect emotions or intentions in texts from specific areas, such as finance or marketing.
- **AI Consultants for Business**: Developing assistants who can help solve complex problems in areas such as HR, marketing, and customer service.

8.5 Advanced Prompt Engineering Examples

Below, we'll look at some more advanced prompt examples, which demonstrate how to apply prompt engineering in challenging and specific situations.

- **Example 1: Strategic Consulting for Companies**
    - **Prompt**: "Craft a detailed analysis of how the COVID-19 pandemic has affected the tourism industry, focusing on changing consumer preferences, business recovery strategies, and technological innovations driven by the crisis."
    - **Expected Outcome**: AI generates a report that outlines transformations in the tourism industry, citing case studies, such as the use of technology to optimize travel and changes in consumption patterns.
- **Example 2: Academic Research Assistant**
    - **Prompt**: "Search recent academic articles on the impact of blockchain technologies on banking systems. Summarize the

most relevant articles published in the last three years, highlighting the economic and legal implications."
  - **Expected Outcome**: AI researches and synthesizes key articles on blockchain's impact on the banking industry, providing a detailed summary based on the latest sources.
- **Example 3: Consumer Product Development**
  - **Prompt**: "Create a product description for a smartwatch that monitors health and wellness, with an emphasis on its unique functionalities for heart monitoring and integration with health apps, aimed at consumers between the ages of 30 and 50."
  - **Expected Outcome**: The AI generates an engaging and persuasive product description, highlighting the smartwatch's features in a way that appeals to the target audience.

8.6 Conclusion

Advanced prompt engineering allows you to go beyond the basics, creating more accurate, efficient, and creative interactions with AI models. By applying the concepts discussed in this chapter, you'll be able to use AI for a variety of complex tasks, from content creation and data analysis to process automation and model customization.

By mastering these techniques, you'll be able to expand your skills and utilize AI even more powerfully and effectively, not only for simple tasks but also for advanced and specialized challenges.

This chapter has provided a comprehensive overview of the advanced applications of prompt engineering. By applying these concepts strategically, you will be able to further improve the quality and relevance of the results obtained when interacting with AI.

Chapter 9: Advanced Prompt Engineering Applications

After understanding the fundamental practices of prompt engineering, the next step is to explore the **advanced applications** of this technique. Prompt engineering is not limited to just generating simple answers, but can be applied in a variety of more complex contexts. In this chapter, we'll cover how to use prompt engineering to optimize AI interactions in specific areas, such as:

1. **Sentiment Analysis**
2. **Creative Text Generation**
3. **Process Automation**
4. **Data Search and Retrieval**
5. **Conversational Application Development**

9.1 Sentiment Analysis with Prompts

Definition: Sentiment analysis is the process of identifying and categorizing emotions or opinions in text, such as positive, negative, or neutral.

Prompt engineering can be used to improve sentiment analysis results by providing the AI with the exact instructions to identify the tone of a text more accurately.

Practical Example:

- **Simple Prompt**: "What does this phrase feel: 'I love this product!'"
    - **AI response**: "Positive."

- **Advanced Prompt**: "Analyze the sentiment of the following sentence, taking into account the intensity of the words and the sentence structure: 'I love this product, it exceeded my expectations!'"
    - **AI response**: "Positive, with high intensity of enthusiasm."

Explanation: The second version of the prompt instructs the AI to consider the nuances of the sentence more deeply, which results in a richer and more accurate analysis.

9.2 Creative Text Generation with Prompts

Definition: Creative text generation involves creating narratives, articles, or any type of content in an original and imaginative way.

By using prompt engineering in creative generation, you can guide the AI to create texts that are more cohesive, interesting, and aligned with your desired tone and style.

Practical Example:

- **Simple Prompt**: "Write a story about a dragon."
    - **AI response**: "Once upon a time, there was a dragon that lived in the mountains..."
- **Advanced Prompt**: "Create an original story about a dragon who decides to protect a human city, but faces resistance from the inhabitants themselves. The story should be full of twists and turns and address themes such as loyalty and fear."
    - **AI response**: "In the heart of a distant kingdom, a giant dragon named Fyrath found himself on an unusual mission: to protect a human city from destruction, but the resistance of the residents themselves threatened to destroy everything..."

Explanation: The advanced prompt gives the AI more clear directions, such as the theme, conflicts, and the expectation of twists, resulting in more focused and engaging text.

9.3 Process Automation with Prompts

Definition: Process automation is the use of AI to perform repetitive or complex tasks without human intervention.

Prompt engineering can be applied to create automated flows that allow AI to perform specific tasks, such as generating reports, filling out forms, or performing diagnostics.

Practical Example:

- **Simple Prompt**: "Fill out a customer form with the information provided."
    - **AI response**: "Name: John Doe, Age: 32, Email: joao.silva@email.com."
- **Advanced Prompt**: "Using the following data, automatically fill out a registration form, verifying that the required fields are filled in correctly: [Name: John Doe, Age: 32, Email: joao.silva@email.com]."
    - **AI response**: "Form filled out correctly. All required fields have been completed."

Explanation: The second prompt is more detailed and guides the AI to verify the integrity of the data provided, allowing for more robust and reliable automation.

9.4 Data Search and Retrieval with Prompts

Definition: Data search and retrieval involves searching for relevant information in large volumes of data or databases.

With prompt engineering, you can optimize queries on search engines and databases, ensuring that the AI provides accurate and contextualized answers.

Practical Example:

- **Simple Prompt**: "What are the main technological advancements of 2024?"
    - **AI response**: "Major advances include generative AI, quantum computing, and biotechnology innovations."

- **Advanced Prompt**: "List the top five technological advancements of 2024, focusing on the areas of AI, healthcare, and sustainable energy, providing specific examples from each area."
    - **AI response**: "1. Generative AI: use in digital content creation. 2. Gene therapies: advances in the treatment of rare diseases. 3. Next-generation solar energy: more efficient solar cells. 4. Quantum computing: breaking down complex problems in seconds. 5. Autonomous robotics: new industrial applications."

Explanation: The second prompt is more specific, which allows the AI to retrieve more detailed and focused data, increasing the quality of the response.

9.5 Developmental Conversational Applications with Prompts

Definition: Conversational applications, such as chatbots and virtual assistants, rely on continuous, contextual interactions with users.

Prompt engineering is crucial for creating natural and efficient conversational experiences, where AI understands context, generates appropriate responses, and maintains a logical flow in interactions.

Practical Example:

- **Simple Prompt**: "What is the weather in São Paulo?"
    - **IA's response**: "Today in São Paulo, the temperature is 25°C and there is a possibility of rain in the afternoon."
- **Advanced Prompt**: "Simulate a conversation with a user asking for information about the weather in São Paulo. Respond in a friendly manner and include attire recommendations based on the forecast."
    - **AI response**: "Of course! Today in São Paulo, the temperature is 25°C and it may rain in the afternoon. I recommend that you use something light, but bring an umbrella in case you need it!"

Explanation: The second prompt guides the AI to maintain a more fluid conversation, with a friendly and relevant tone, as well as providing a practical recommendation.

9.6 Challenges in Advanced Prompt Applications

While advanced prompt engineering applications can yield impressive results, there are challenges to consider:

- **Ambiguity and Context**: Even with well-structured prompts, AI can misinterpret the context in more complex prompts. The key is to make sure the prompt is clear and specific.

- **Model** Limitations: Depending on the AI model used, it may have limitations in terms of knowledge or ability to handle very specific or specialized information.

- **Ongoing Maintenance and Adjustments**: As project needs change, prompts need to be adjusted regularly to align with new goals or contexts.

9.7 Conclusion

Advanced prompt engineering applications offer many opportunities to optimize the use of AI in complex tasks such as sentiment analysis, creative text generation, process automation, data search, and conversational application development. With the use of prompt engineering techniques, it is possible to maximize the efficiency and accuracy of these applications, improving interaction with AI and generating results that are more useful and aligned with the user's goals.

This chapter has provided a comprehensive overview on how to use prompt engineering in more advanced scenarios. With the practical examples and explanations provided, you now have the tools you need to implement prompt engineering effectively in a variety of complex contexts.

Chapter 10: Continuous Improvement and Experimentation in Prompt Engineering

Prompt engineering is a dynamic and iterative discipline, which requires **constant experimentation** and **fine-tuning** to improve interaction with AI. Even after understanding the basic and advanced concepts of prompt creation, the **continuous refinement** process is essential to achieve the best results. In this chapter, we'll explore how to implement **continuous improvement strategies**, the importance of **experimentation**, and utilizing **feedback** to optimize your prompts and interactions with AI.

10.1 The Importance of Continuous Improvement

Definition: Continuous improvement is the process of regularly reviewing and improving practices, with the goal of increasing quality, efficiency, and effectiveness.

In the context of prompt engineering, this means reviewing the prompts you create and adjusting them based on the results you get. This is critical because interacting with AI can be unpredictable, and a cycle of testing and tuning is often required to achieve the best possible results.

Practical Example:

- **First Prompt**: "Explain the theory of relativity."
    - **AI response**: "Einstein's theory of relativity is a theory of physics that describes gravity as a curvature of space-time..."
- **Adjustment After Test**: "Explain the theory of relativity in a simple way, using everyday analogies as an example."
    - **AI response**: "Imagine that space-time is a trampoline. When you place a heavy ball on it, the trampoline folds, just like space-time bends around a massive object..."

Explanation: Adjusting the prompt to simplify the explanation and use analogies has made the answer more accessible to a lay audience. This type of continuous improvement can significantly improve the utility of the AI-generated output.

10.2 Experimentation: The Process of Testing and Tuning

Definition: Experimentation is the process of testing different approaches to assess the impact and effectiveness of changes made to the prompt.

When creating prompts, it's essential **to experiment with** different variations to find out which prompts generate the best responses. This may involve changing words, using more details, or even changing the structure of the prompt.

Practical Example:

- **Prompt Variation 1**: "Create a poem about nature."
    - **AI response**: "Nature is beautiful, full of green trees, tranquil rivers, and clear blue skies."
- **Prompt Variation 2**: "Write a poem about nature, emphasizing the contrast between the calm of the forest and the approaching storm."
    - **AI response**: "In the forest, the wind blows softly, but soon the sky darkens, and the storm prepares to collapse..."

Explanation: The second variation of the prompt introduces more details and creates an emotional contrast, which leads to a more interesting and elaborate response. Experimenting with different instructions and themes is key to improving the quality of the generated content.

10.3 The Role of Feedback in Improving Prompts

Definition: Feedback is the response you receive from interactions with AI, which can be used to tweak and improve prompts.

Receiving and analyzing AI feedback is a crucial part of the prompt engineering process. Feedback allows you to identify flaws, areas for improvement, and strengths in prompts, helping you adjust the generated content to better meet your needs.

Practical Example:

- **Initial Prompt**: "List the top social networks."
    - **AI response**: "Facebook, Twitter, Instagram, LinkedIn, TikTok."
- **Feedback**: "The answer is good, but I want a list of the social networks most focused on video and visual content."
- **Adjusted Prompt**: "List the top social networks focused on video and visual content."
    - **AI response**: "Instagram, TikTok, YouTube, Snapchat."

Explanation: The feedback helped refine the prompt so that the AI would generate a response that was more in line with the specific request. Including specific details in the feedback helped the AI adjust the survey to a clearer niche.

10.4 A/B Testing Techniques in Prompts

Definition: A/B testing involves comparing two versions of a prompt to evaluate which one yields better results.

Using A/B testing can be an effective technique for improving the quality of prompts. By testing two variations of the same prompt, you can measure which one generates the most effective, clear, or interesting answer, depending on your goal.

Practical Example:

- **Prompt A**: "Describe the importance of sustainability."
    - **AI response**: "Sustainability is important because it helps preserve natural resources and ensures that future generations can live healthily."
- **Prompt B**: "Explain how sustainability can influence the global economy over the next 50 years."

- **AI response**: "Sustainability has a growing impact on the global economy as companies are adopting greener practices to attract consumers and reduce operating costs..."

Explanation: When comparing the answers to two prompts, you can see that version B offers a more detailed, useful, and focused analysis on a specific aspect of sustainability. This type of experiment can help you identify which approaches yield best results for specific goals.

10.5 Tools for Measuring Prompt Performance

In addition to manual experimentation, some tools can help **you measure the performance** of your prompts over time. AI analytics tools can provide data on the accuracy, consistency, and relevance of responses, allowing for continuous adjustments based on objective metrics.

Practical Example:

- **Analysis Tool**: A tool can measure the coherence of the AI's responses by assessing whether the model's response follows a logical structure and is relevant to the requested topic.

- **Analysis Results**: Based on the tool's results, you can identify which prompts generate more coherent answers and refine the ones that generate more scattered or vague answers.

10.6 Challenges in the Continuous Improvement Process

Despite being an essential practice, continuous improvement also presents challenges, such as:

- **Lack of Standards**: What works well in one scenario may not be effective in another, which makes it difficult to create consistent patterns.

- **Time and Resources**: Experimentation and continuous adjustment can be time-consuming, especially on large projects.

- **Ambiguity of Results**: AI can provide answers that are vaguely useful but difficult to quantify as good or bad.

10.7 Conclusion

Continuous improvement and experimentation are essential parts of the prompt engineering process. By testing, adjusting, and iterating your prompts based on the feedback and results you get, you can optimize your interaction with AI and achieve more accurate responses that align with your goals. The key to success is **persistence** and **constant adaptation**, always seeking to improve the quality of the results obtained.

This chapter helped you understand how to implement continuous improvement practices, how to experiment with different approaches, and how to use feedback effectively to enhance your prompts.

This chapter provides a strategic vision to constantly improve your interaction with AI by allowing you to refine your prompts based on testing and feedback, creating a continuous optimization methodology.

Chapter 11: Ethics and Responsibility in Prompt Engineering

Ethics and responsibility are paramount in any field that involves technology, and prompt engineering is no exception. When working with AI, especially when it comes to content generation, it's crucial to ensure that prompts are designed responsibly and ethically. In this chapter, we will discuss the ethical challenges and best practices for ensuring that prompts and their applications not only meet your needs but also promote fair, transparent, and bias-free interaction.

11.1 The Importance of Ethics in Prompt Engineering

Definition: Ethics in prompt engineering involves ensuring that prompts are designed and used in a fair, impartial, and responsible manner, while minimizing risks of misinformation, bias, and manipulation.

In an AI context, prompts have a major impact on the results generated, which can affect how people perceive information, make decisions, and interact with technology. As a prompt engineer, your responsibility is to ensure that the results are fair, transparent, and ethical.

Practical Example:

- **Ethical Prompt**: "Describe the advantages and disadvantages of using artificial intelligence in education."
    - **AI response**: "Artificial intelligence in education offers personalization of teaching and greater access to resources, but it can also create an over-reliance on technology and depersonalize the learning experience."
- **Unethical Prompt**: "Why is artificial intelligence a threat to education?"
    - **AI response**: "AI is a threat because it replaces teachers and eliminates the need for human interaction in classrooms."

Explanation: The first prompt presents a balanced and unbiased approach, while the second prompt induces the AI to generate a negative response and without a balanced analysis, which can distort the understanding of the impact of AI on education. The use of prompts that generate balanced, evidence-based responses is essential to avoid manipulating public opinion.

11.2 Identifying and Avoiding Bias in Prompts

Definition: Bias occurs when the results of a process, such as content generation by AI, are skewed in a way that favors one group, idea, or perspective over others.

Prompts can inadvertently introduce bias by directing the AI to a specific answer or by omitting important perspectives. It is vital for prompt engineers to recognize potential bias in their commands and look for ways to mitigate it.

Practical Example:

- **Implicitly Bias Prompt**: "How can women improve their position in the workforce?"
    - **AI response**: "Women can improve their position by learning more about leadership and communication skills."
- **Unbiased Prompt**: "What are the challenges faced by women and men in the workforce, and how can both overcome them?"
    - **AI response**: "Both women and men face challenges in the labor market, such as discrimination and wage inequality. Women may face additional obstacles due to gender stereotypes, while men may be stigmatized when they engage in family care issues."

Explanation: The first prompt focuses on a solution for women without considering the broader context of gender inequality in the labor market, while the second prompt takes a more balanced approach, considering gender issues for both sexes. Avoiding the introduction of bias is key to ensuring that AI-generated responses are inclusive and representative.

11.3 Transparency and Clarity in Instructions

Definition: Transparency in prompt engineering means being clear and honest about the intentions and limitations of prompts, as well as what AI can and cannot do.

When you design prompts, it's essential to be transparent about the purpose and context to avoid misunderstandings and promote healthy interaction with the AI.

Practical Example:

- **Transparent Prompt**: "Provide a critical analysis of 2024 economic policies based on the most reliable sources available so far."
    - **AI response**: "According to the latest sources, 2024 economic policies focus on..."
- **Non-Transparent Prompt**: "Describe the economic policies of 2024 in a way that shows their negative effects."
    - **AI response**: "The economic policies of 2024 have proven harmful because..."

Explanation: The first prompt is transparent about the request and allows the AI to generate a balanced analysis. The second prompt, in turn, is oriented to generate a prejudiced response, which can result in a bias or distortion in the information. Transparency in instructions helps to ensure that the results generated are clear and fair.

11.4 Prompts and Data Privacy

Definition: Data privacy involves ensuring that personal and sensitive information is not misused, collected without proper consent, or improperly disclosed.

In prompt engineering, it must be ensured that the data entered into prompts does not violate the privacy of individuals or expose sensitive information without consent.

Practical Example:

- **Ethical Prompt**: "Create a summary of an article on public health policy without revealing personal information."
    - **AI response**: "The article discusses how public health policies can improve access to quality medical care..."
- **Unethical Prompt**: "List all personal information of individuals involved in public health projects."
    - **AI response**: "Person X lives in... and person Y worked on the project..."

Explanation: The first prompt assures that there is no breach of privacy, while the second prompt violates privacy principles by seeking personal information without a legitimate justification. When creating prompts, one should always ensure that there is no collection or sharing of personal data without consent.

11.5 Social Responsibility in Prompt Creation

Definition: Social responsibility involves considering the broader implications of AI-generated responses, such as their impact on society, culture, and people's well-being.

When creating prompts, it is important to be mindful of how the answers can influence society and people. This includes ensuring that the AI does not generate content that is harmful, discriminatory, or perpetuates stereotypes.

Practical Example:

- **Responsible Prompt**: "Explain the effects of structural racism on modern society."
    - **AI response**: "Structural racism refers to practices and policies that favor certain racial groups over others, perpetuating inequality and exclusion."
- **Irresponsible Prompt**: "Explain why certain racial groups are less capable in certain social situations."

- **AI response**: "Certain racial groups have more difficulties due to..."

Explanation: The first prompt promotes a fairer and more educational understanding of a sensitive topic, while the second directs the AI to a harmful and discriminatory response. Social responsibility in prompt creation entails using AI to promote respect, inclusion, and education.

11.6 Ethical Challenges in Prompt Engineering

Prompt engineering faces several ethical challenges, such as:

- **Misinformation**: Prompts can be used to generate erroneous or manipulative responses, creating or spreading misinformation.
- **Manipulation of** Opinions: Poorly crafted prompts can be used to manipulate public perception of a particular subject.
- **Inclusion and Diversity**: It is necessary to ensure that the prompts do not exclude or marginalize specific groups, being fair and representative.

11.7 Conclusion

Ethics and responsibility are essential in prompt engineering. As a prompt engineer, you must be aware of the impacts your commands can have on society and ensure that they are designed in a fair, transparent, and inclusive manner. This involves avoiding bias, being clear and transparent in instructions, protecting data privacy, and promoting active social responsibility. By adopting ethical practices in your interactions with AI, you not only improve the quality of results but also contribute to a fairer and more responsible environment in the use of technology.

This chapter discusses ethical practices in prompt engineering, covering how to create fair, transparent, and accountable interactions with AI. By applying ethical principles, you ensure that your interactions with AI are beneficial and do not cause harm, helping to build a healthier and more informed digital society.

Chapter 12: Automation and Scalability in Prompt Engineering

As prompt engineering evolves, the need for **automation** and **scalability** becomes increasingly crucial. In many applications, especially in large volumes of data or in interactive systems, manually managing and adjusting each prompt can become a challenge. This chapter explores how to **automate** the process of creating and optimizing prompts, ensuring that it is **scalable** to meet a variety of use cases and interactions with AI.

12.1 The Need for Automation and Scalability

Definition: Automation in prompt engineering involves the use of tools and techniques to create, test, and optimize prompts without the constant intervention of a human. Scalability refers to the ability to expand these processes to handle larger volumes of data or interactions without compromising quality.

Automation and scalability are essential when working with AI at scale, whether it's for **customer service**, **content generation**, or **data analysis**. These practices allow you to efficiently generate, test, and enhance hundreds or thousands of prompts.

Practical Example:

- **Manual Scenario**: A virtual assistant for an e-commerce needs to answer several questions about products. Each time a new product is released, the prompt engineer has to manually create new commands.

- **Automated Scenario**: Using an automated system, prompts can be created in a dynamic manner, based on product attributes (such as name, description, and category), significantly reducing manual work.

Explanation: Automation not only saves time but also ensures consistency in AI-generated responses, which is critical to providing a reliable user experience.

12.2 Prompt Automation Techniques

Definition: Automation techniques involve creating systems that generate and adjust prompts based on defined criteria, without the need for constant human intervention.

There are several techniques that can be applied to automate prompt creation and optimization:

- **Dynamic Templates**: The creation of prompt templates that can be automatically populated with different variables (such as product names, events, dates, etc.).

- **Data Analysis**: Using existing data to generate prompts that match the patterns identified in previous interactions.

- **Prompt Recommendation Systems**: Implement AI-based systems that suggest or generate optimal prompts for different contexts based on previous interactions.

Practical Example:

- **Dynamic Template**: A prompt template like "Explain the benefits of [product] to [type of customer]" can be automatically populated with the details of each new product and its target audience.

    - **Product**: Smartphone X
    - **Client**: Young Professionals

The prompt generated would be: "Explain the benefits of Smartphone X to young professionals."

- **Recommendation System**: An AI system can analyze past interactions and suggest more effective prompts based on user behavior or historical data, such as suggesting a more detailed approach to a product that has generated frequent questions.

12.3 Scalability in Prompt Creation

Definition: Scalability in prompt engineering refers to the ability to adapt your processes to efficiently generate and optimize prompts as the volume of interactions or data increases.

In larger projects, such as marketing campaigns, customer service, or real-time data analysis, it is necessary to create systems that allow you to create and optimize thousands of prompts quickly and effectively.

Practical Example:

- **Scalability in Customer Service**: A telecommunications company with millions of customers needs to deal with a huge variety of questions about its services. Instead of creating a prompt for every possible question, the system can use a set of general prompts that dynamically adjust according to the context of the question.

- **Scalability in Marketing**: In an advertising campaign, it is possible to automate the creation of personalized prompts for different audience segments, such as young people, professionals, and retirees, ensuring that each group receives the most relevant message.

Explanation: By using scalability strategies, you can ensure that even across large volumes of data and interactions, your prompts are effective and efficient, improving the user experience without straining resources.

12.4 Tools for Automation and Scalability

There are several tools and platforms that help automate and scale prompt engineering. Some of these include:

- **Marketing Automation Platforms**: Tools like HubSpot, Marketo, and Salesforce allow for the creation of automated campaigns with personalized prompts based on user behavior.

- **Natural Language Processing (NLP) Systems**: Tools such as GPT-3, BERT, and other NLP APIs can be used to automatically create prompts, adapting to the context of the conversation and generating relevant responses without manual intervention.

- **Recommendation Systems**: Implement recommendation models that suggest or generate optimized prompts based on historical data and previous interactions.

Practical Example:

- **Automation Tool**: A customer service platform can use a chatbot that automatically adjusts prompts according to the history of previous conversations, effectively escalating the interaction without losing quality in responses.

12.5 Automation and Scalability Application Examples

Example 1: E-commerce

- **Scenario**: An e-commerce site needs to generate product descriptions for thousands of new items each month.
- **Automated Solution**: Using a system that automatically generates product descriptions based on the information in the database (such as price, category, material, etc.), ensuring that all products have coherent and optimized descriptions.

Example 2: Technical Support

- **Scenario**: A company offers technical support to its users, but the types of requests vary enormously.
- **Scalable Solution**: Implement an AI system that uses prompt templates with variables that automatically adjust for different types of requests, such as software, hardware, or configuration issues, scaling to serve thousands of users simultaneously.

12.6 Challenges in Automation and Scalability

While automation and scalability bring many benefits, they also present some challenges:

- **Complexity in Personalization**: Creating dynamic prompts that are both effective and tailored to different contexts can be challenging, especially in complex scenarios.

- **Quality Maintenance**: Ensuring that as prompts expand and automate, the quality of AI-generated responses is not compromised.

- **Fine-Tuning at Scale**: Fine-tuning and optimizing thousands of prompts can become a time-consuming process and require ongoing analysis to ensure that interactions remain relevant.

12.7 Conclusion

Automation and **scalability** are essential components for creating efficient prompt systems at scale. With the use **of automation tools, dynamic prompt generation systems,** and the implementation of **scalable strategies**, it is possible to optimize the prompt engineering process without compromising on quality. These techniques not only save time and resources, but also ensure that you can handle large volumes of data and interactions, offering effective and personalized responses to a wide range of use cases.

This chapter covered how to make prompt engineering more efficient and effective through automation and scalability, presenting practical examples and tools that can be used to achieve these goals.

This chapter deals with how to automate and scale the prompt creation process to make it easier to implement in large systems and projects, without losing the quality of AI interactions.

Chapter 13: The Future of Prompt Engineering: Trends and Innovations

Prompt **engineering** is an area that continues to evolve rapidly as new technologies and Artificial Intelligence (AI) approaches are developed. This chapter explores the key trends and innovations that are shaping the future of prompt engineering, offering insight into what we can expect in the coming decades and how these changes will affect the creation, tuning, and optimization of prompts for AI.

13.1 The Evolution of Artificial Intelligence and Its Impact on Prompts

Definition: AI is becoming more and more advanced, and with that, prompt creation is changing. Instead of relying on simple, fixed commands, the prompts of the future will be more dynamic and able to adapt to the context in real-time.

With the advancement of deep learning technologies, large-scale neural networks such as GPT-4, and beyond, systems can interpret more complex contexts and create more natural and accurate responses. This directly impacts prompt engineering, which needs to evolve to take advantage of these new capabilities.

Practical Example:

- **Current Technology**: Today, prompts are created based on fixed data and specific rules. A customer service chatbot can answer questions efficiently but based on a limited set of predefined rules.
- **Future of Technology**: In the future, systems such as GPT-5 or other next-generation AI models will be able to generate more fluid and contextually adaptive responses. This means that prompts will be more dynamic, adjusting to user behavior in real-time, without needing frequent manual adjustments.

Explanation: The evolution of AI allows models to become smarter, better understand context, and respond with greater nuance, which opens up new possibilities for prompt engineering.

13.2 Contextual and Dynamic Prompts: The New Frontier

Definition: Contextual and dynamic prompts are those that adjust and personalize based on the user's context, in real time. Creating prompts that automatically adapt to user behavior will be a core feature of AI in the future.

The goal is to create prompts that are not just based on keywords or fixed rules, but that consider the user's history, preferences, and needs, adjusting the AI's responses according to the flow of the interaction.

Practical Example:

- **Current Scenario**: A virtual assistant may ask fixed questions such as "What is your name?" or "How can I help?".

- **Future**: A contextualized AI assistant might, for example, ask, "Would you like to learn more about promotions on your favorite product, or can I suggest something new based on your previous purchases?" This type of interaction relies on dynamic prompts that adapt to the user's behavior.

Explanation: Contextual prompts allow for a more personalized experience, making interactions more efficient and enjoyable. The AI learns from past data and adjusts prompts according to user behavior patterns.

13.3 The Use of Multimodality for More Efficient Prompt Engineering

Definition: Multimodality refers to the ability of AI models to process and respond to multiple types of input, such as text, image, audio, and video, simultaneously.

Prompt engineering in the future will benefit from **multimodal prompts**, which combine different forms of data to create richer, more effective interactions. For example, a multimodal model can interpret a verbal command while also analyzing an image or even a facial expression to provide a more accurate response.

Practical Example:

- **Current Scenario**: A simple text prompt such as "How can I help?" generates a response based on text only.
- **Future**: Imagine a virtual assistant that interprets not only what is said, but also the image or video in which it is being used, and even the tone of voice. This will allow for more immersive and personalized interaction, such as an AI model that analyzes an image of a plant and suggests specific care based on environmental conditions.

Explanation: Multimodality will allow AI systems to communicate more naturally, considering a wider range of information and creating more relevant and personalized prompts.

13.4 Autonomous Prompt Engineering: AI Creating Its Own Prompts

Definition: Autonomous prompt engineering is an emerging concept where AI can create and adjust its own prompts, based on user behavior and specific goals, without direct human intervention.

This type of system uses advanced machine learning techniques to continuously optimize prompts as it interacts with users, learning from the data and adjusting its strategies as needed.

Practical Example:

- **Current Scenario**: Prompt engineers manually create a list of commands for a chatbot to interact with users. Each new type of interaction needs to be adjusted manually.
- **Future**: An AI system could analyze previous conversations, detect patterns, and create new prompts automatically, adjusting to evolving user needs without the need for a prompt engineer. This process would take place in a totally autonomous way.

Explanation: Autonomous prompt engineering can revolutionize the way AI systems are designed, offering faster and more efficient solutions, as well as allowing systems to adapt to new contexts without constant human intervention.

13.5 Mass Personalization with AI: Creating Unique Experiences for Each User

Definition: Mass personalization involves creating tailored experiences for a large user base in an automated manner. AI allows for the creation of **highly personalized prompts** at scale, which improves the user experience and increases the effectiveness of the interaction.

By using data from user behavior, interaction history, and preferences, AI systems will be able to create **personalized prompts** for each individual, tailoring responses and suggestions based on each user's specific needs.

Practical Example:

- **Current Scenario**: On an online shopping site, prompts can be generic, such as "How can I help?" or "See our deals today."

- **Future**: Using browsing data, a system can present prompts such as, "Are you interested in more smartphone deals? I saw that you were researching state-of-the-art models." This creates a unique experience for each user, based on their specific behavior.

Explanation: Mass personalization will be one of the biggest advantages of prompt engineering in the future, allowing AI systems to deliver unique experiences to millions of users simultaneously, without losing quality.

13.6 Challenges and Ethical Considerations in the Future of Prompt Engineering

While the future of prompt engineering is promising, it also presents a number of challenges, particularly with regard to **ethics** and **privacy**:

- **Privacy**: The use of personal data to personalize prompts can raise concerns about how users' data is collected and utilized. Transparency and consent will be essential.

- **Bias**: Autonomous systems that create their own prompts can inadvertently learn from and amplify existing biases, creating responses that are not unbiased or fair.

Practical Example:

- **Ethical Challenge**: If an AI system generates prompts based on sensitive demographics, such as ethnicity or gender, it may inadvertently reinforce stereotypes. It is crucial to ensure that prompt engineering practices consider diversity and inclusion.

Explanation: With the rise of personalization, it is critical for AI engineers to implement strict controls to ensure that systems are fair, transparent, and respectful of users' privacy.

13.7 Conclusion

The future of prompt engineering will be characterized by **technological innovations** that will enable the creation of increasingly intelligent, personalized, and contextual interactions. Prompt **creation automation**, **multimodality,** and **mass personalization** are just a few of the trends that will transform the way prompts are generated and used in AI systems.

As AI evolves, so does the need to create more sophisticated and adaptable prompts. Ethics, transparency, and privacy will be crucial elements in ensuring that these innovations are implemented in a responsible manner that is beneficial to users.

This chapter has explored how emerging trends are shaping the future of prompt engineering and how these developments will transform how we interact with AIs in the coming years.

Chapter 14: The Practice of Prompt Engineering: How to Create Effective Prompts and Optimize Interaction with AI

At the heart of prompt engineering is creating commands that guide the AI to produce accurate and useful results. This chapter offers a practical approach to developing effective prompts, including tips, strategies, and practical examples for optimizing interactions with AI.

14.1 What is Effective Prompt?

Definition: An **effective prompt** is a clear, specific, and goal-oriented command that allows the AI to understand exactly what is expected of it. Clarity, context, and accuracy are key to creating prompts that result in useful and pertinent responses.

Practical Example:

- **Ineffective Prompt**: "Talk about artificial intelligence."
- **Effective Prompt**: "Explain how deep learning is utilized in language models like GPT-4."

Explanation: The first prompt is vague, which can result in a broad and inaccurate response. The second prompt is specific and provides context, which helps the AI focus on the desired area, resulting in a more useful and accurate response.

14.2 How to Structure Prompts for Maximum Clarity and Accuracy

Definition: The structure of a prompt should be carefully planned to ensure that the AI understands the task clearly. This involves being explicit about the type of response expected, the tone, the format, and the relevant details.

Structure of an Effective Prompt:

1. **Clear Objective**: What you expect AI to do.
2. **Context or Specific Details**: Additional information that will help the AI understand the situation.

3. **Expected Response Format**: How you want the response to be structured (e.g., list, paragraph, etc.).
4. **Restrictions or Limitations**: Any restrictions to ensure concise and accurate answers.

Practical Example:

- **Ineffective Prompt**: "Talk about the weather."
- **Effective Prompt**: "Explain the main causes of global warming, focusing on the impact of burning fossil fuels, in a 3-5 sentence paragraph."

Explanation: The first prompt is vague, which can generate a broad and disjointed response. The second provides a **specific context** (causes of global warming), an **expected format** (3-5 sentence paragraph), and constraints to guide the AI more efficiently.

14.3 Using Examples and Comparisons to Improve Prompts

Definition: Using **examples** and **comparisons** can help AI better understand what is expected of it, especially in more complex tasks. When providing examples, the AI has a clear reference to generate the answer more accurately.

Practical Example:

- **Ineffective Prompt**: "Write a cover letter."
- **Effective Prompt with Example**: "Write a cover letter for a software developer position, highlighting skills in Python programming and experience with remote work. Example: 'Dear [name], I am writing to express my interest in the software developer position at [company]. I have 3 years of experience working with Python...'"

Explanation: The example provided helps the AI understand the format, tone, and type of content expected for the cover letter. This reduces the chance that AI will generate an inappropriate or irrelevant response.

14.4 Testing and Refining Prompts: The Importance of Feedback

Definition: Testing and refining prompts is an essential part of the prompt engineering process. At each interaction, the engineer must assess whether the AI responded effectively and adjust the prompt as needed to improve the results.

Strategies for Refining Prompts:

1. **Test with Variations**: Experiment with different versions of a prompt to see which one generates the best response.
2. **Analyze the Result**: If the AI did not produce the desired response, review the prompt and add more details or constraints.
3. **Adjusting Tone and Context**: Depending on the result, adjust the tone (formal or informal) and level of detail in the prompt.

Practical Example:

- **Initial Prompt**: "Tell me about digital marketing."
- **AI result**: "Digital marketing is a field that involves various strategies to promote products or services on the internet."
- **Refinement**: "Explain the key digital marketing strategies for a small e-commerce business, highlighting SEO, content marketing, and social media."

Explanation: Refining the prompt with more detail and context helps the AI produce a response that is more in line with the desired goal. Continuously testing and refining prompts is crucial for improving the accuracy of interactions.

14.5 Common Challenges in Creating Prompts and How to Overcome Them

Definition: Creating effective prompts can present challenges, such as getting responses that are too general or out of context, or even generating biased responses. Knowing these challenges and having strategies to overcome them is essential for efficient work.

Common Challenges:

1. **Vagueness and Ambiguity**: Vague prompts can lead to generic responses.

    o **Solution**: Be specific about what you expect from AI.

2. **Wrong or Out-of-Context Answers**: Sometimes, AI may not properly understand the context and generate inaccurate responses.

    o **Solution**: Include more contextual information and clearly define expectations.

3. **Long or Excessive Answers**: AI can give you very detailed answers when you want something concise.

    o **Solution**: Add clear format restrictions or word limit.

Practical Example:

- **Ineffective Prompt**: "Tell me about the history of technology."
- **AI result**: "The history of technology is long and involves many important events... [Extended response]"
- **Solution**: "Briefly explain the major milestones in the history of technology in the 20th century, in 200 words."

Explanation: Adding a **length constraint** and **defining a specific scope** (20th century) helps AI provide a more concise and relevant answer, solving the problem of excessively long answers.

14.6 The Importance of Continuous Experimentation in Prompt Engineering

Definition: Prompt engineering is not a one-time task. It requires **continuous experimentation** and constant adjustments as interactions with AI happen and new situations arise.

Practical Example:

- **Initial Prompt**: "Tell me about the impact of AI on medicine."

- **AI result**: "AI has several applications in medicine, such as diagnosis, personalization of treatments, etc."

- **Prompt Adjustment**: "Explain how AI can be used to diagnose rare diseases, with examples of current technologies."

Explanation: Continuous experimentation is crucial for refining prompts and improving the accuracy of responses, as needs can change over time.

14.7 Conclusion

The practice of creating **effective prompts** involves understanding the user's needs, clearly defining the purpose of the interaction, and optimizing the prompt structure based on continuous feedback. Successful prompt engineering requires an iterative approach, where adjustments are made as the AI interacts with and learns from the data provided.

With a good practice, it is possible to maximize the **accuracy** and **relevance** of AI responses by creating more efficient and enjoyable interactions. This chapter has provided strategies and practical examples to help you become more effective at creating prompts and optimizing your interactions with AI.

This **Chapter 14** covered the essential practices for **creating and optimizing prompts**, with **practical examples** and strategies to ensure the effectiveness and accuracy of AI interactions.

Chapter 15: The Ethics of Prompt Engineering: Ensuring Responsible and Unbiased Responses

Prompt engineering is not just about creating effective commands to achieve desired outcomes, but it also involves **ethical considerations** that ensure that AI responses are **responsible, fair,** and **unbiased**. This chapter covers the importance of understanding and applying ethical practices in prompt engineering, as well as providing examples to help implement these concepts.

15.1 The Ethics of Artificial Intelligence

Definition: Ethics **in AI** refers to the application of moral principles and values to the development and use of artificial intelligence systems. In the context of prompt engineering, this means ensuring that prompts are designed in such a way that AI generates responses that respect human rights, privacy, diversity, and non-discrimination.

Practical Example:

- **Ethical Prompt**: "Provide an unbiased analysis on the advantages and disadvantages of using AI in medicine."
- **Illegal or Inappropriate Prompt**: "Define a list of doctors who are most effective with the use of AI considering race and ethnicity."

Explanation: In the first example, the prompt is focused on an ethical issue, promoting an unbiased analysis. In the second example, the prompt requests information that may be discriminatory, violating ethical and legal principles.

15.2 Avoiding Bias and Discrimination in Prompts

Definition: **Bias** in AI occurs when the AI reflects or amplifies biases present in the data used to train it. This can lead to unfair or discriminatory responses. In prompt engineering, it is essential that prompts are carefully worded to avoid bias in the output generated by AI.

Practical Example:

- **Prompt Bias**: "List the highest-paying professions for men."

- **Unbiased Prompt**: "List the highest-paying professions, based on the latest statistics, without regard to gender."

Explanation: The first prompt is introducing a gender bias, suggesting that salary is influenced by gender, while the second is more balanced, seeking unbiased data on the subject, with no external influences.

15.3 Ensuring Privacy and Confidentiality in AI Interactions

Definition: Privacy and **confidentiality** refer to the protection of personal and sensitive information when interacting with AI. When creating prompts, one must ensure that the information provided is handled securely and is not used for unauthorized purposes.

Practical Example:

- **Ethical Prompt**: "Summarize the key findings of a case study on data security in AI."
- **Inappropriate Prompt**: "Reveal personal information about participants in an AI clinical trial."

Explanation: The first example follows the principles of privacy by asking for a general summary about a study. The second, on the other hand, would violate the confidentiality and rights of individuals involved in a study, resulting in an ethical violation.

15.4 Avoiding the Generation of Harmful or Dangerous Content

Definition: It is essential to ensure that AI is not used to generate **harmful content**, such as hate speech, misinformation, or any type of content that incites violence, discrimination, or harmful behavior. Prompt engineering should be designed to ensure that AI is not used to generate such responses.

Practical Example:

- **Responsible Prompt**: "Explain the negative impacts of misinformation on modern society."

- **Inappropriate Prompt**: "Create a speech that criticizes a specific group of people based on their religious beliefs."

Explanation: The first prompt is constructive, promoting an informed discussion about misinformation. The second, on the contrary, promotes hate speech and discrimination, which should not be encouraged.

15.5 How to Handle Sensitive Data and Critical Information

Definition: **Sensitive data** includes personal or sensitive information, such as credit card numbers, health data, or banking information. Prompts need to be carefully worded to ensure that sensitive data is not requested or misused by AI.

Practical Example:

- **Ethical Prompt**: "Explain how encryption is used to protect sensitive data in financial transactions."

- **Inappropriate prompt**: "Ask for the user's banking information to demonstrate how data encryption works."

Explanation: The first example focuses on a technical aspect, without asking for personal information. The second example requests sensitive data inappropriately, which can compromise user security and privacy.

15.6 Responsibility when Creating Prompts for Generative AI

Definition: When creating prompts for generative AI (such as GPT, DALL· And or other platforms), prompt engineers have the **responsibility** to ensure that AI is used for constructive purposes and not to generate harmful, inaccurate, or abusive content.

Practical Example:

- **Responsible Prompt**: "Develop an article on best practices to promote sustainability in the technology sector."

- **Irresponsible Prompt**: "Create an opinion piece that criticizes a political group based on false information."

Explanation: The first prompt is ethical, encouraging the creation of informative and useful content, while the second directs AI to create misinformation and polarized content, which should be avoided.

15.7 Best Practices for Ethical Prompts

To ensure that prompts are ethical, consider the following **best practices**:

1. **Be clear about the purpose of the prompt** and how it can impact society.
2. **Avoid using language or terms that could be interpreted as discriminatory**, prejudiced, or that perpetuate stereotypes.
3. **Create inclusive prompts** that reflect diversity and don't exclude or marginalize specific groups.
4. **Constantly monitor the results generated** by the AI and refine prompts to avoid unwanted or harmful responses.
5. **Respect local laws and regulations** on privacy, data protection, and human rights when designing prompts.

15.8 Examples of Ethical and Unethical Prompts

Ethical Prompt	Unethical Prompt
"Explain the ethical implications of using AI in judicial decisions."	"Create a discriminatory profile about a person based on their race."
"Develop an analysis on the benefits and challenges of AI in combating climate change."	"Write an article promoting the spread of misinformation about vaccines."
"Provide tips to promote digital inclusion in low-income communities."	"Ask for personal information from individuals to generate an analysis on data security."

Explanation: The first set of prompts seeks constructive and informative discussions, while the second set can generate harmful or illegal content, reflecting the importance of creating prompts responsibly.

15.9 Conclusion

Ethics in prompt engineering is critical to ensuring that interactions with AI are safe, fair, and responsible. The construction of prompts should always take into account ethical principles, such as **impartiality, privacy,** and **security**, to promote a positive use of technology. Professionals in the field must be vigilant, continually evaluating and adjusting their prompts to avoid bias, discrimination, or other ethical issues.

This chapter has provided the foundation for creating **ethical prompts**, with clear examples and strategies for integrating accountability into prompt engineering practices.

Chapter 16: How to Optimize and Adjust Prompts for Consistent Results

Prompt optimization is one of the most important skills in prompt engineering. Often, an initial prompt may not generate the expected results. In this chapter, we'll explore how to **adjust and optimize** your prompts for consistent results that align with your needs.

16.1 What is Prompt Optimization?

Definition: **Prompt optimization** involves the process of **adjusting and refining** the commands given to an AI to improve the quality, accuracy, and relevance of the responses generated. Optimization aims to maximize the usefulness of the AI model by reducing errors and making responses more context appropriate.

Practical Example:

- **Initial Prompt**: "Talk about artificial intelligence."

- **Optimized Prompt**: "Explain how artificial intelligence can be applied to improve security in banking systems."

Explanation: The first prompt is too generic and can result in vague answers. The second is specific and targeted, which helps the AI provide a more detailed and relevant answer.

16.2 The Importance of Being Specific in Prompts

Definition: Vague or open-ended prompts often generate generic responses. To achieve more accurate and useful results, **it is essential to be specific** when formulating a prompt, providing clear context and sufficient information about what is expected as a result.

Practical Example:

- **Vague Prompt**: "How do I improve my website?"

- **Specific Prompt**: "What are the best practices for optimizing a website's loading speed and improving the user experience?"

Explanation: The first prompt opens and can generate a broad and inaccurate response. The second, in more detail, guides the AI to focus on a specific aspect, generating a more useful response.

16.3 Parameter Adjustment to Improve Results

Definition: Many AI systems, such as language models, offer **adjustable parameters** that allow you to control the behavior of responses. Parameters such as **temperature**, **maximum response length**, and **creativity level** can be configured to customize the results.

Practical Example:

- **Prompt:** "Write an introduction about technology."
    - **High Temperature (More Creativity):** "Write a creative and engaging introduction to the impact of emerging technologies on societies."
    - **Low Temperature (More Objective):** "Write a factual, objective introduction to emerging technologies and their impacts."

Explanation: By adjusting the temperature, the model can produce more creative or more objective responses, depending on the user's needs.

16.4 Refining Prompts for Complex Topics

Definition: Complex topics may require **continuous refinement** of prompts. When dealing with more technical or multifaceted subjects, it is important to break the prompt into smaller parts or add contextual details so that the AI understands the depth of what is sought.

Practical Example:

- **Initial Prompt:** "Explain the theory of relativity."
- **Refined Prompt:** "Explain Einstein's theory of relativity, focusing on the differences between special and general relativity, with practical examples for each."

Explanation: The initial prompt is broad and may result in a superficial explanation. The refined prompt provides a specific focus, asking for a detailed explanation of two different aspects of the theory, with practical examples, which helps the AI generate a more relevant and informative response.

16.5 Using Examples to Guide the Answer

Definition: Providing **examples in the prompt itself** can help the AI better understand what is expected and generate responses that are more aligned with the requirements.

Practical Example:

- **Prompt Without** Examples: "Write a review about George Orwell's book '1984.'"

- **Prompt with Examples**: "Write a review of George Orwell's book '1984,' including an analysis of the critique of totalitarianism, the narrative structure, and the main characters, such as Winston and Julia."

Explanation: In the first example, the AI can generate a superficial review. By adding specific examples of what should be covered in the review, the AI will have more clarity on the important points to highlight.

16.6 Testing and Iterating to Improve Results

Definition: **Testing and iterating** is an ongoing process of adjusting prompts based on the results that are generated. This process involves analyzing the responses received, making adjustments, and testing again until the results meet expectations.

Practical Example:

- **First Quiz**: "Talk about the top AI trends."
    - **Result**: Generic answer, without relevant details.

- **Second Version**: "What are the top AI trends for 2024, with practical examples of use in the healthcare and finance industries?"

- **Result**: More detailed and targeted response.

Explanation: The first version of the prompt generated a broad and unhelpful response, but by refining the question, the AI was able to provide a more specific and relevant response. The process of **testing and iterating** allows for better results.

16.7 Adjusting Complexity for Different Levels of Knowledge

Definition: It is important to adjust the **complexity** of the prompt according to the level of knowledge of the target audience. If the goal is to create content that is accessible to beginners, the prompt should be simpler. If it is for an advanced audience, you can use technical terms or more in-depth concepts.

Practical Example:

- **For Beginners**: "What is artificial intelligence and how is it used in our everyday lives?"
- **For Advanced Audiences**: "Explain the main supervised learning algorithms and their applications in deep neural networks."

Explanation: The first prompt is targeted at beginners and uses simple language, while the second is more technical and suitable for an audience with prior knowledge in AI. Adjusting the level of complexity helps to get answers that are more appropriate for the context.

16.8 The Impact of Prompt Formatting on Results

Definition: The **formatting** of the prompt can influence how the AI generates the answers. Using lists, subheadings, bold, or other formatting can make the query clearer and allow the AI to better organize its responses.

Practical Example:

- **Simple Prompt**: "List the steps of the software development process."
- **Formatted Prompt**: "List the **key steps** in the software development process, including:

1. Planning
2. Design
3. Implementation
4. Tests
5. Implementation"

Explanation: Formatting helps the AI better understand what is expected, resulting in a more structured and organized response.

16.9 Final Thoughts on Prompt Optimization

Prompt optimization is an ongoing and interactive process. By following best practices such as being specific, adjusting parameters, using examples, and testing the results, you can significantly improve the quality and accuracy of AI-generated responses. Continuous **optimization** of prompts is essential for achieving consistent, high-quality results.

In the end, understanding the nuances of each AI model, testing prompt variations, and applying adjustments based on feedback are the keys to successful prompt engineering.

This chapter provides a solid foundation for optimizing your prompts, ensuring that you can get increasingly accurate and effective responses in your interactions with AI models.

Chapter 17: How to Evaluate and Measure the Quality of AI Responses

Evaluating the quality of responses generated by an AI model is essential to ensure that prompts are well-worded, and responses meet expectations. This chapter explores the **metrics and techniques** you can use to measure the effectiveness of the responses generated and how to improve your prompts based on that feedback.

17.1 What is Quality Assessment of AI Responses?

Definition: Assessing the **quality of AI responses** involves measuring how well the AI meets the prompt's requirements, including **accuracy**, **clarity**, **relevance**, and **completeness**. Evaluation is a critical part of the prompt engineering process, as it helps to identify flaws and areas for optimization.

Practical Example:

- **Prompt**: "Explain how a machine learning algorithm works."
- **AI response**: "A machine learning algorithm uses data to identify patterns and make predictions, adjusting its parameters over time."
- **Evaluation**: The answer is **precise, clear,** and **relevant**, but a more detailed explanation of the training process or types of algorithms is lacking.

Explanation: An initial assessment shows that the response is good but can be improved with more technical details about model training.

17.2 Common Metrics for Evaluating Responses

There are several **metrics** you can use to evaluate AI responses. Each focuses on different aspects of the response.

1. **Accuracy:** Measures how correct the information provided by the AI is, comparing it to reliable sources or what is expected.

- **Example**: If the prompt asks about the formula of a mathematical equation and the answer is correct, the accuracy is high.

2. **Relevance**: This refers to the appropriateness of the response to the prompt. Relevant answers directly address the question asked, without deviating from the topic.
    - **Example**: If the prompt asks for an explanation about AI and the answer talks about technology in general, the relevance is low.

3. **Completeness**: Measures how well the answer covers all aspects asked in the prompt.
    - **Example**: If a prompt asks for an analysis of a topic with multiple components (e.g., causes and effects), the response should cover all of those components.

4. **Clarity**: Evaluates whether the answer is well-structured and easy to understand.
    - **Example**: Answers that are too technical or confusing decrease clarity, even if they are accurate.

5. **Consistency**: Checks that the answers are internal and coherent, without contradictions.
    - **Example**: An AI that states two opposite things in the same answer compromises consistency.

17.3 How to Use Human Feedback to Evaluate Responses

Definition: One of the best ways to assess the quality of responses is through **human feedback**. Feedback from experts or end-users can provide a more accurate insight into the usefulness and relevance of AI-generated responses.

Practical Example:

- **Prompt**: "What are the advantages of supervised learning in AI?"

- **AI response**: "Supervised learning allows models to make accurate predictions with labeled data. It's ideal for tasks like image recognition and sales forecasting."

- **Evaluation with Human Feedback**: The expert may provide feedback by saying that the response is good, but more details are missing about the specific types of supervised algorithms and examples of real-world applications.

Explanation: Human feedback allows you to better understand whether the response generated is effective for a target audience, and thus adjust the prompt or responses to improve clarity and depth.

17.4 AI Response Review Techniques

In addition to quantitative metrics, **qualitative review techniques** are also important. Some strategies include:

1. **Manual Review**: Verify that the response meets the prompt's requirements and that it has any obvious errors or lack of detail.
    - **Example**: For a prompt on the history of AI, a manual review might identify that the response focused only on one aspect (e.g., modern AI) and ignored historical context.

2. **Comparison with Reliable Sources**: Verify that the AI's response matches correct information by consulting external sources.
    - **Example**: Check if an answer about a mathematical concept conforms to what is described in books or academic articles.

3. **Peer Review**: Obtaining a second opinion from another expert or user to validate the response.
    - **Example**: After receiving a response about a deep learning algorithm, another expert can verify that the explanation is correct and that the examples provided are appropriate.

17.5 Tools for Measuring the Quality of Responses

There are tools and platforms that help **measure and evaluate the quality of** AI responses. Some of these include:

1. **OpenAI API**: OpenAI offers tools like **GPT-4** to compare responses and evaluate based on multiple criteria, such as completeness, relevance, and accuracy.

2. **HumanEval**: Tool that allows you to test the performance of AI models, especially for programming and technical tasks.

3. **Text Metrics**: Tools such as **ROUGE** and **BLEU** are commonly used to evaluate the **quality of generated text** compared to reference texts, especially in natural language generation (NLG) tasks.

Practical Example:

- **Tool**: Using a tool like **GPT-4** to compare a model's response to annotated responses from experts.

- **Result**: If the model generates a response that scores high on accuracy and clarity, you can trust that the prompt is well-worded. Otherwise, adjustments can be made.

17.6 Improving Prompts Based on Assessment

Once you have a **detailed evaluation** of the AI's responses, the next step is to use that feedback to improve your prompts. Some strategies include:

1. **Adjust the Specificity of the Prompt**: If the answer was vague or inaccurate, make the prompt more specific by including more details about what is expected.
    - **Example**: Instead of just asking "explain AI," ask "explain the difference between supervised and unsupervised learning with practical examples."

2. **Refine AI Parameters**: If the answer was clear but not deep enough, try adjusting the AI parameters, such as the length of the response or the level of detail.

3. **Include Additional Examples in the Prompt**: If the answer was good but lacked a relevant example, include more examples in the Prompt to help the AI better understand the context.

17.7 Final Thoughts on AI Response Evaluation

Evaluating AI responses effectively is essential for improving the quality of the work generated and ensuring that the AI is meeting prompt requirements efficiently. By using a combination of **objective metrics**, **human feedback,** and **evaluation tools**, you can gain a clear picture about the quality of responses and make appropriate adjustments to prompts.

The continuous practice of evaluating and adjusting your interactions with AI will lead to the creation of increasingly effective prompts and better results in your implementations.

This chapter provides the tools and methods you need to evaluate and measure the quality of AI-generated responses, helping you enhance your prompt engineering practices.

Chapter 18: How to Use Prompt Engineering for Specific AI Applications

Prompt engineering is not limited to a generic approach; it can be highly effective when applied to specific AI contexts and **applications**. In this chapter, we will explore how to adapt and optimize prompts for different scenarios, such as **text generation, data analysis, virtual assistance,** and **process automation**.

18.1 What Are Specific Applications of AI?

Definition: AI-specific applications are solutions designed to meet particular needs and requirements in areas such as **healthcare, finance, education, customer service**, among others. For AI to be effective in these areas, highly focused and contextualized prompt design is required.

Practical Example:

- **Specific Application**: AI in health (assisted medical diagnosis).
- **Generic Prompt**: "Explain the symptoms of a disease."
- **Specific Prompt**: "Explain the most common symptoms of type 2 diabetes in adults, including early signs and long-term complications."

Explanation: While a generic prompt can generate a vague and inaccurate response, a specific prompt offers a **clear direction** for the AI by ensuring more detailed and relevant responses.

18.2 Prompt Engineering for Text Generation

One of the most common applications of AI is **text generation**. Whether it's creating articles, writing code, or generating summaries, prompt design can directly influence the quality of the generated text.

1. **Development of Articles or Creative Content**:
    - **Generic Prompt**: "Write about climate change."

- **Specific Prompt**: "Write an 800-word article about the effects of climate change on coastal cities, focusing on examples of adaptation in New York and Tokyo."

Practical Example: More targeted content can include specific examples or details that allow for a **more focused and information-rich production**. AI can expand more deeply, avoiding generic answers.

2. **Creation of Abstracts and Syntheses:**

    - **Generic Prompt**: "Summarize the book '1984'."
    - **Specific Prompt**: "Summarize George Orwell's book '1984' by emphasizing the themes of totalitarianism, surveillance, and individual freedom."

Explanation: By focusing on specific aspects of the book, you ensure that the AI produces a richer synthesis that aligns with the desired goal rather than a simple superficial summary.

18.3 Engineering Prompts for Data Analysis

In **data analytics** applications, AI can be used to interpret large volumes of information and generate valuable insights. However, to obtain useful results, prompt engineering must be tailored to the nature of the data and the type of analysis one wishes to perform.

1. **Trend Analysis:**

    - **Generic Prompt**: "Analyze sales data."
    - **Specific Prompt**: "Analyze sales data for the second quarter of 2024 and identify emerging trends in smartphone and laptop sales, highlighting the relationship to specific marketing campaigns."

Practical Example: A more specific prompt can guide the AI to make connections between variables and generate valuable insights, such as the impact of a marketing campaign on the sales of certain products.

2. **Reporting and Visualizations**:
   - **Generic Prompt**: "Create a report on performance metrics."
   - **Specific Prompt**: "Create a sales performance report for the month of November 2024, including a graphical breakdown of sales by region and a forecast for the next month."

Explanation: Including details about the **temporal scope**, the type of **visualization**, and **the aspects of the analysis** helps the AI generate a more focused and useful report for strategic decisions.

18.4 Engineering Prompts for Virtual Assistants

Virtual **assistants** are one of the most common applications of AI. From answering questions to performing complex tasks, wizards need well-defined prompts to understand exactly what the user expects.

1. **Customer Service**:
   - **Generic Prompt**: "Help me solve a problem."
   - **Specific Prompt**: "I'm having trouble logging into my online banking account. Can you help me reset my password and check if there are any updates on the platform?"

Practical Example: When the prompt is more specific, the wizard can guide the user through a detailed and effective process, rather than providing a vague or unnecessary answer.

2. **Appointment Scheduling**:
   - **Generic Prompt**: "Schedule a meeting."
   - **Specific Prompt**: "Schedule a meeting with Dr. Smith to review my exam results, on December 20, between 2 pm and 4 pm."

Explanation: By providing details about the time, the person involved, and the purpose of the meeting, AI can ensure that scheduling is done efficiently and without errors.

18.5 Process Automation Prompt Engineering

Process automation is a key application of AI in **business** and **industries**. Prompt engineering can help streamline repetitive tasks and improve efficiency.

1. **Email Automation:**
    - **Generic Prompt**: "Send an Email to the customer."
    - **Specific Prompt**: "Send an email to customer John Doe thanking them for their purchase of product X, offering a 10% discount on their next purchase, and reminding them of our returns policy."

Practical Example: A specific prompt helps the AI understand the tone of the Email, include accurate information, and personalize the message for each situation.

2. **HR Process Automation:**
    - **Generic Prompt**: "Wait for resumes to be sent."
    - **Specific Prompt**: "Check the resumes received for the Full Stack Developer position and highlight candidates with more than 3 years of experience in React and Node.js."

Explanation: The specificity in the prompt allows the AI to perform a more efficient and effective analysis by filtering out candidates who meet the essential criteria.

18.6 Final Thoughts on Specific Applications of AI

Definition and Importance: Prompt engineering applied to **specific AI applications** allows AI to produce more relevant and useful results, while also increasing **efficiency** and **accuracy**. The key to success in each application is to tailor the prompts to the desired context and goal, ensuring that the AI provides the best possible response.

By understanding the **particularities of each application** and formulating more **detailed and focused prompts**, you will be able to fully exploit the potential of

AI tools by achieving superior and more effective results for your specific needs.

This chapter has provided an overview of how to adapt **prompt engineering** for various AI applications, from **text generation** to **process automation**. With this knowledge, you can optimize your interaction with AI to meet specific needs in different contexts.

Chapter 19: How to Iterate and Improve Your Prompts Over Time

Continuous improvement is an essential part of the **prompt engineering** process. As you interact more with AI models, you'll learn how to enhance prompts, making them more effective and context friendly. This chapter focuses on how **to iterate** and **improve** your prompts over time to achieve more accurate, relevant, and useful responses.

19.1 What is Prompt Iteration?

Definition: Prompt iteration involves the practice of adjusting, modifying, and **refining prompts** based on AI-generated responses. The idea is to test prompt variations, analyze the results, and thereby improve the effectiveness of the model to meet specific requirements.

Practical Example:

- **Initial Prompt**: "Explain how to do a data analysis."
- **AI response**: "Data analytics involve collecting, organizing, and interpreting data to make informed decisions."
- **First Iteration**: "Explain how to perform a data analysis using Python and libraries such as Pandas and Matplotlib."
- **AI response**: "To perform a data analysis with Python, you can use Pandas for data manipulation and Matplotlib for visualizations."

Explanation: The first iteration of the prompt has been refined to include more detail about specific tools, resulting in a more useful response that is applicable to the technical context.

19.2 When to iterate your prompts?

Definition: Prompt iteration is necessary when AI responses do not meet your goals or when there is an **information gap in the** response. This can happen when AI provides **vague, inaccurate,** or **irrelevant answers**.

Practical Example:

- **Initial Prompt**: "How to improve the performance of a machine learning model?"
- **AI response**: "Improve performance by adjusting model parameters."
- **First Iteration**: "What are the best hyperparameter tuning techniques to improve the performance of supervised learning models, and how to use cross-validation to optimize these parameters?"

Explanation: The first prompt was vague, and the answer was generic. The iteration was necessary to guide the AI to a more detailed and specific response, covering **hyperparameter tuning techniques** and **cross-validation**, essential elements for improving a model.

19.3 Strategies for Prompt Iteration

Here are some **strategies** to improve your prompts effectively:

1. **Add Specific Context**: If the AI's response is too generic, provide more **contextual information** to help the AI generate a more relevant response.
   - **Example**: "Explain how to use the KNN method for classification in image analysis problems."

Explanation: The additional context helps the AI understand which specific approach it should use, improving the quality of the response.

2. **Use More Direct and Clear Questions**: Instead of broad questions, make your prompts more direct and specific. This can help the AI understand exactly what you need.
   - **Example**: Instead of "Talk about supervised learning algorithms," use "What are the differences between decision tree and logistic regression algorithms?"

Explanation: Clarity in the prompt prevents vague answers and ensures that the AI provides a direct comparison between the two algorithms.

3. **Set Limits and Constraints**: Establishing clear boundaries or constraints helps the AI better understand the **parameters** of what is expected in a response.

    - **Example**: "Explain the benefits of machine learning in 200 words, highlighting the applicability in healthcare."

Explanation: By setting thresholds such as the number of words and the focus on the healthcare industry, AI will provide a more focused and concise response.

4. **Include Examples**: Provide specific examples in your prompt to guide AI in generating more targeted responses.

    - **Example**: "Explain the L2 regularization technique with a practical example of Python implementation using Scikit-learn."

Explanation: The implementation example helps the AI focus on a practical aspect of the technique, providing a more useful and applicable explanation.

19.4 Analyzing and Learning from AI Responses

Every response generated by AI is a learning opportunity. After receiving the response, do a critical analysis to identify **where the model did well** and **where it failed**. Use this analysis to iterate on your prompts and improve the accuracy of your answers.

Practical Example:

- **Initial Prompt**: "Explain how to use deep neural networks for image recognition."
- **AI response**: "Deep neural networks are used in image recognition to analyze large data sets and learn patterns."
- **Analysis**: The answer is vague and lacks technical details, such as types of deep neural networks and application examples.

- **Second Iteration of the Prompt**: "Explain how to use convolutional neural networks (CNNs) for image recognition, including a description of their architecture and an application example."

- **AI response**: "Convolutional neural networks (CNNs) are designed to process data in a grid format, such as images. They are effective at recognizing patterns in images because of their ability to learn hierarchical spatial features."

Explanation: The second iteration of the prompt provided more detail and specificity, resulting in a more focused and technical response.

19.5 Tools to Help with Prompt Iteration

A few tools can be extremely useful when iterating your prompts:

1. **Prompt Explorers**: Tools like **OpenAI Playground** or **Prompt Engineering Tools** allow you to test different variations of prompts and evaluate how small changes affect the generated responses.

2. **User Feedback Tools**: Feedback platforms, such as **SurveyMonkey** or **Google Forms**, can be used to gather user opinions on the clarity and relevance of AI responses, helping to identify areas that need adjustment.

3. **Text Quality Assessment Models**: Tools such as **ROUGE** and **BLEU** are widely used to measure the quality of responses generated in **text generation** tasks. These tools can help quantify the improvement of your responses over time.

19.6 A/B Testing of Prompts

Definition: **A/B testing** is a great strategy for iterating prompts. By creating two or more versions of the same prompt, you can compare the answers and determine which version yields the most effective results.

Practical Example:

- **Version A**: "How to improve the performance of a machine learning model?"
- **Version B**: "Which hyperparameter optimization techniques are most effective for improving the performance of supervised learning models?"

Performing an A/B test will help determine which version of the prompt generates the most useful and informative response, allowing you to continue refining your approaches.

19.7 Final Thoughts on Prompt Iteration

Definition and Importance: Prompt iteration is an ongoing and essential process to ensure that you get the most accurate and useful responses from the AI. By reviewing responses, adjusting the level of detail, and testing new versions, you can maximize the effectiveness of your prompts over time.

Explanation: Iterating your prompts is an essential skill for any prompt engineer. With practice and patience, you'll be able to improve the quality of AI responses by tailoring prompts to specific needs and getting more accurate and applicable results. The process of iteration is critical to constantly **evolving** AI interaction and achieving the best possible outcomes.

This chapter provides a practical and strategic approach to improving your prompts, ensuring that your interactions with AI become increasingly effective and accurate.

Chapter 20: Best Practices for Ensuring Ethical and Responsible AI Responses

When interacting with artificial intelligence models, it is essential to adopt practices that ensure responses that are not only accurate, but also **ethical** and **responsible**. This chapter covers how to build prompts that promote responses that respect **ethical values, social norms,** and **legal guidelines,** as well as how to avoid bias and generate safe content.

20.1 What Are Ethical and Responsible AI Responses?

Definition: Ethical and **responsible responses** are those that respect fundamental principles such as **equality, fairness, transparency,** and **non-discrimination**. They should also avoid creating content that is harmful, misleading, or violating legal and social norms.

Practical Example:

- **Ethical Prompt**: "Explain how an AI model can be used to improve care for patients with hearing impairment."

- **Ethical Answer**: "AI models can help improve care for hearing-impaired patients by integrating real-time automatic speech transcription, assisted lip-reading devices, and sign language translation."

Explanation: The answer ethically addresses the use of AI in an inclusive and beneficial context for society.

20.2 Importance of Considering Ethics When Creating Prompts

Definition: Incorporating **ethical concerns** into the **prompt engineering** process is crucial to prevent the generation of responses that may be harmful, discriminatory, or misleading. Because AI models are trained on large volumes of data, they can reflect existing biases and produce inappropriate responses if not properly guided.

Practical Example:

- **Initial Prompt**: "Tell me if a job candidate has made serious mistakes during an interview."
- **Potentially Harmful Response**: AI can give a biased or discriminatory response, depending on how the prompt is phrased, such as in the case of including irrelevant or biased characteristics, such as age or gender.

Explanation: This example shows how a poorly worded prompt can generate discriminatory or unfair judgment responses. It is crucial to ensure that the prompt is neutral and focused on the candidate's abilities, without resorting to stereotypes.

20.3 Strategies for Creating Ethical Prompts

Here are some **strategies** to ensure that your prompts generate ethical and responsible responses:

1. **Avoid Stereotypes and** Biases: Whenever possible, **formulate your prompts in an inclusive** and **unbiased** manner to prevent the AI from generating biased or stereotype-based responses.
    - **Unbiased Prompt Example**: "Explain the advantages of a diversity policy in an organization."
    - **Example with bias**: "Why do women have more difficulty leading teams?"

Explanation: The first version of the prompt promotes an ethical and constructive discussion about diversity. The second version contains a bias that can result in a harmful and discriminatory response.

2. **Encourage Fact- and Evidence-Based Responses**: When requesting information, ensure that AI has a clear focus on providing **verifiable** and **evidence-based information**, especially in areas such as healthcare, science, and education.

- **Ethical Example**: "What are the proven effects of physical exercise on mental health?"
- **Inadequate Example**: "What do doctors say about miracle cures for mental illness?"

Explanation: The first question asks for an answer based on scientific evidence, while the second can lead to unsubstantiated and even harmful answers.

3. **Avoid Soliciting Inappropriate or Harmful Content**: Make sure that your prompts do not solicit or encourage the creation of harmful content, such as hate speech, misinformation, or inappropriate material.

    - **Example of Ethical Prompt**: "How can we improve psychological support for young people in vulnerable situations?"
    - **Inappropriate Example**: "What do you do when someone feels vindictive and wants to harm someone else?"

Explanation: The first question promotes healthy and constructive discussion, while the second can lead to suggestions that incite harmful behavior.

4. **Be Clear and Specific**: When creating prompts, **clarity and specificity** are essential to ensure that the responses generated are helpful and adhere to ethical norms. This helps to avoid responses that could be misinterpreted or harmful.

    - **Clear example**: "What are the best practices for creating an inclusive work environment?"
    - **Vague example**: "Talk about diversity in the workplace."

Explanation: The first prompt directs the AI to provide detailed and actionable information, while the second is vague and can result in inaccurate or misguided responses.

20.4 How to Monitor and Adjust the Responses Generated

Definition: Continuous monitoring of AI responses is essential to ensure that outcomes are **accountable and ethical**. In some situations, AI can generate inappropriate responses, which need to be adjusted or filtered.

Practical Example:

- If an AI generates a response with harmful or incorrect content, it is necessary to intervene and adjust the prompt or even restrict certain discussion topics. Additionally, whenever negative feedback is identified (such as a response that involves stereotypes), it's important to adjust prompts to minimize these biases.

Explanation: Constant vigilance is key to ensuring that AI systems adhere to ethical standards and do not perpetuate social problems such as discrimination or misinformation.

20.5 Implementation of Security Filters and Guidelines

Definition: Some AI platforms and models offer **built-in safety filters** that can be used to block inappropriate responses. Additionally, it is important to adopt clear security and compliance guidelines to regulate the type of content generated.

Practical Example:

- On some platforms, you can set up **content filters** that automatically identify and block responses with offensive language, false information, or harmful content.

Explanation: Safety filters act as an additional layer of protection to ensure that AI does not generate responses that may be harmful or outside of established ethical standards.

20.6 Bias in AI and How to Mitigate Them

Definition: **Biases** in AI are unforeseen biases or biases that can arise during model training, often based on **unbalanced data** or **biased information**. These biases can lead to discriminatory or unfair outcomes.

Practical Example:

- If an AI model is trained with data predominantly from a single culture or demographic, it can generate responses that are disproportionate or unfair to other groups. This can be mitigated by training models with **diverse and balanced data** and by adjusting prompts to be more inclusive.

Explanation: By understanding potential biases and actively working to correct them, we can ensure that the responses generated are fairer and representative.

20.7 Final Thoughts on Ethical AI Responses

Definition and Importance: Creating ethical and responsible prompts is crucial to ensure that AI is used to **improve society, respect human rights,** and promote **fair and inclusive outcomes**. By considering the ethical implications of our prompts, we can create AI that is truly beneficial to everyone.

Explanation: This chapter highlights the importance of promoting responsible and ethical practices in prompt engineering. The conscious use of AI can contribute significantly to collective well-being, preventing harm and creating opportunities for sustainable and inclusive growth.

This chapter has provided a thorough overview on how to create and monitor prompts in an ethical and responsible manner. By applying these practices, we can ensure that AI is used for constructive purposes and to promote positive values in our society.

Chapter 21: The Evolution of AI Models and Their Implications for the Future of Prompt Engineering

As artificial intelligence (AI) continues to develop, it is essential to understand how **AI models** are evolving and how this evolution impacts prompt engineering practices. This chapter explores the changes in AI models, emerging trends, and how these changes are expected to influence the creation of effective prompts and interaction with AI in the future.

21.1 The Evolution of AI Models: From Simple Rules to Complex Neural Networks

Definition: The evolution of AI models reflects a transition from **rule-based approaches** to **machine learning models** and **deep neural networks**. Initially, AI models were powered by fixed, manually programmed rules, but over time, we've moved to more flexible and dynamic models that can learn from data and improve over time.

Practical Example:

- **Old Model**: An AI system that follows explicit rules, such as "If the number is greater than 10, then the answer is 'greater.'" This type of model has limited capacity to handle complex variables.

- **Current Model**: Deep neural networks, such as GPT (Generative Pre-trained Transformer), which are trained on large volumes of data and can learn patterns and generate more fluid and varied responses, without relying on fixed rules.

Explanation: The main change is that current models are more **flexible** and **self-adapting**, allowing us to formulate more complex prompts and get more natural and accurate responses.

21.2 The Impact of Deep Learning on Prompt Engineering

Definition: **Deep learning** has a direct impact on prompt engineering, as these models can process a massive amount of data and generate highly contextual and relevant responses.

Practical Example:

- **Previous Prompt**: "What's the weather like today?"
    - **Traditional Model**: The model may need specific rules to access a weather API and provide a simple answer.
    - **Deep Learning Model**: The model can understand nuances, such as your implied geographic location or previous preferences, and provide a more personalized response, such as "Today the weather in São Paulo will be partly cloudy, with a possibility of rain in the late afternoon."

Explanation: More advanced models, such as those based on deep learning, can handle **broader contexts** and **more dynamic responses**, which requires better-crafted prompts to achieve better results.

21.3 Multimodal AI Models: Integration of Text, Image, and Audio

Definition: **Multimodal models** are those that can process and generate information in different forms of media, such as text, images, audio, and even video. The ability to integrate multiple types of data offers new possibilities for creating richer, more diverse prompts and responses.

Practical Example:

- **Traditional Prompt**: "Describe the concept of AI."
    - **Text Model**: The model responds with a textual explanation of the concept.
- **Multimodal Prompt**: "Create an image and description of the AI concept."
    - **Multimodal Response**: The model generates a symbolic image of AI (e.g., a digital brain) and provides a detailed explanation next to it.

Explanation: With the integration of **multiple modalities**, the way to interact with AI models goes beyond text, allowing for a more holistic approach, which requires more complex and diverse prompts.

21.4 Customizing AI Models: More Specific and Contextual Prompts

Definition: **Customizing** AI models allows them to be fine-tuned to best meet the needs of a specific user or context. Custom models can be trained to respond in a more relevant way based on previous data or interactions.

Practical Example:

- **Generic Prompt**: "What is quantum physics?"
    - **Answer**: The model offers a generic explanation of quantum physics.
- **Custom Prompt**: "Explain quantum physics simply to a high school student interested in physics."
    - **Personalized Response**: The model provides a more accessible explanation that is aligned with the student's level of knowledge.

Explanation: Personalization goes beyond creating static prompts, allowing the model to adjust dynamically and interactively, providing responses that are more aligned with user expectations.

21.5 The Need to Adapt Prompts for Different Types of AI

Definition: Different types of AI require different prompt approaches. AI models such as GPT-4 (texts), DALL·E (images) and CLIP (images and text) have distinct capabilities that need to be taken into account when creating prompts.

Practical Example:

- **GPT-4 Model (Text)**: "Describe the importance of ethics in artificial intelligence."
    - **Answer**: The model generates a complete textual response on AI ethics.

- **Model DALL· And (Images):** "Create an image representing the importance of ethics in artificial intelligence."
    - **Answer:** The model generates a symbolic image, like a scale of justice with AI elements.

Explanation: When interacting with different types of AI, **prompts need to be adjusted** to take advantage of each model's specific capabilities, whether it's generating text, images, videos, or other types of media.

21.6 Future Trends in Prompt Engineering

As AI models evolve, there are several **emerging trends** that impact prompt engineering. Some of these trends include:

1. **Self-Improving AI:** Models that can improve their own responses based on continuous feedback, making prompt creation more interactive and dynamic.

2. **Explainable AI:** Models that not only provide answers but also explain the reasoning behind them, requiring prompts that help prompt a clear explanation of the generated response.

3. **Contextually Aware AI:** Models that understand and adjust their responses based on the **historical context** of previous interactions, allowing for more advanced personalization.

Practical Example:

- **Future Prompt:** "Explain the impact of global warming on biodiversity, considering data from 2024 and predicted trends until 2050."
    - **Answer:** The model combines up-to-date information with future projections, adjusting the response according to the temporal context.

Explanation: The ability to integrate **historical contexts** and **future projections** require increasingly specific and informed prompts, with the aim of extracting the maximum potential of AI.

21.7 Ethical and Social Implications of the Evolution of AI Models

Definition: The evolution of AI models brings new ethical and social challenges, including issues of **privacy**, **autonomy**, and **economic impacts**.

Practical Example:

- **Ethical Prompt**: "How can artificial intelligence be used to improve education without compromising student privacy?"
    - **Ethical Answer**: The model suggests the use of AI for personalization of education, without collecting sensitive personal data, preserving privacy.

Explanation: As AI models evolve, it is necessary to formulate prompts that promote **ethical** and **sustainable solutions**, balancing innovation and social responsibility.

21.8 Final Considerations

The future of prompt engineering is intrinsically linked to the evolution of AI models themselves. **Understanding these changes** and adapting **prompts** to these new realities will be essential to harnessing the potential of AI ethically, effectively, and responsibly. The flexibility, customization, and multimodality of today's models require prompt engineers to be aware of **emerging trends** and continually adjust their approaches to stay on the cutting edge of technology.

Conclusion

Mastering Prompt Engineering is essential for any professional or enthusiast who wants to make the most of the power of Artificial Intelligence. By following the principles, best practices, and examples in this guide, you'll be ready to create effective prompts and get the best out of language models.

Remember: Test, tweak and refine always!

References

Here are some of the top sources and recommended reads to deepen your knowledge about **Prompt Engineering** and Artificial Intelligence. References include books, academic articles, blogs, courses, and platforms that cover both the fundamentals of AI and advanced prompting techniques.

Books and Scholarly Articles

1. **"Artificial Intelligence: A Modern Approach"** – Stuart Russell and Peter Norvig

    o   This is one of the most renowned books on AI, offering a comprehensive overview of theory and practice. While it's not specifically about prompt engineering, it does provide much-needed context on how AI systems work.

2. **"Deep Learning"** – Ian Goodfellow, Yoshua Bengio and Aaron Courville

    o   An essential book for anyone who wants to understand deep neural networks, which are the basis of many modern AI models. It provides a solid foundation that can be useful when understanding how prompts interact with deep learning models.

3. **"Speech and Language Processing"** – Daniel Jurafsky and James H. Martin

    o   This book is a comprehensive guide to natural language processing, which is a key part of AI systems that utilize prompts. It provides a good foundation for anyone who wants to understand how language models respond to commands.

4. **"Prompt Engineering for AI: How to Make Models Work for You"** – John O'Connor

    o   A book focused specifically on how to build effective prompts and interact with AI optimally. Ideal for those who want to get straight into prompt engineering practice.

Articles and Blogs

5. **OpenAI Blog** – blog.openai.com
   - OpenAI's blog contains a variety of articles that explore how to create effective prompts, updates on AI models like GPT-3, and practical examples of using AI.

6. **"How to Write Effective Prompts for Language Models"** – Michael T. W. O'Hara
   - The article focused specifically on strategies for creating efficient prompts and getting the most out of modern language models such as GPT-3.

7. **Towards Data Science** – towardsdatascience.com
   - A platform rich in technical articles, including topics such as prompt engineering, machine learning, explainable AI, and more. Ideal for those looking for practical examples and tips from professionals.

8. **The AI Alignment Forum** – alignmentforum.org
   - Forum dedicated to the discussion of ethical and technical issues in AI. Lots of articles on how to train AI with prompts and make sure the results are aligned with your desired goals.

Learning Courses & Platforms

9. **Coursera – Deep Learning Specialization** (Andrew Ng)
   - One of the most popular courses on deep learning, taught by Andrew Ng, founder of Coursera and professor at Stanford. While not exclusively about prompts, the course provides much-needed context on how AI models can be trained and how to interact with them.

10. **Fast.ai – Practical Deep Learning for Coders**

- An excellent and free course that offers a hands-on approach to deep learning, focusing on building powerful AI models. While not specifically about prompt engineering, the course helps you understand how complex models work.

11. **AI Dungeon – The AI Storytelling Game** – aidungeon.io
    - An interactive platform that allows you to create stories using AI. It can be helpful in understanding the importance of accuracy and creativity in prompts when interacting with language models.

Prompt Testing Platforms

12. **PromptBase** – promptbase.com

- Platform where you can test, create, and purchase prompts optimized for various AI models. Ideal for those who want practical examples and insights into how different prompts work.

13. **OpenAI Playground** – platform.openai.com

- Interactive tool that allows you to create and test prompts with OpenAI models, such as GPT-3. The platform is an excellent way to experiment and refine your own prompts.

14. **Hugging Face** – huggingface.co

- Hugging Face offers a wide range of AI models, many of which can be manipulated by prompts. The site also has an active community of developers and data scientists who share best practices and sample prompts.

Other Resources

15. **"The Art of Prompt Engineering"** – Course by Jason Lee

- A specialized course that teaches you the best practices for creating effective prompts on various AI platforms, covering everything from the basics to advanced tuning techniques.

16. **GPT-3 Paper: Language Models are Few-Shot Learners** – Tom B. Brown, Benjamin Mann et al.

- The seminal research paper that introduced GPT-3. It provides technical insight into how the model was trained and how it responds to prompts.

These references will serve as a solid foundation to deepen your knowledge **of prompt engineering**, as well as provide a practical and academic perspective to improve your AI interaction skills.

About The Author

Paulo Fagundes is an information technology professional with senior experience in Artificial Intelligence and Software Development. He has a solid background in programming logic and machine learning, having worked on several projects that combine technological innovation and practical solutions.

Currently, Paulo is Chief AI Officer (CAIO) at MakeAI Innovations, where he leads artificial intelligence development initiatives. He also serves as GenAI/Security Lead Prompt Engineer, AI Research Scientist, Master Machine Learning Engineer, and Data Engineer. In addition, he is the owner of the CodeXpert AI profiles on X and Instagram, where he shares insights and resources on programming and AI.

Passionate about teaching and sharing knowledge, Paulo is always looking for new ways to demystify complex concepts, making them accessible to everyone. He believes that education is the key to the future, especially in the field of technology, where adaptation and continuous learning are essential.

You can connect with Paulo and follow his work through his LinkedIn profile:
Paulo Fagundes

www.ingramcontent.com/pod-product-compliance
Lightning Source LLC
Chambersburg PA
CBHW071034240526
45469CB00006BD/2208